Dracula's Army

Andy Fish

McFarland & Company, Inc., Publishers
Jefferson, North Carolina, and London

ALSO BY ANDY FISH

Werewolves of Wisconsin and Other American Myths, Monsters and Ghosts (McFarland, 2012)

LIBRARY OF CONGRESS CATALOGUING-IN-PUBLICATION DATA

Fish, Andy.
Dracula's Army : the Dead Travel Fast / Andy Fish.
p. cm.

ISBN 978-0-7864-7582-7

softcover : 50# alkaline paper ♾

1. Vampires—Comic books, strips, etc. 2. Shapeshifting—Comic books, strips, etc. 3. Graphic novels. I. Stoker, Bram, 1847–1912. Dracula. II. Title.
PN6727.F576D73 2014 741.5'973—dc23 2013036516

BRITISH LIBRARY CATALOGUING DATA ARE AVAILABLE

Cover illustration by Andy Fish

Manufactured in the United States of America

McFarland & Company, Inc., Publishers
Box 611, Jefferson, North Carolina 28640
www.mcfarlandpub.com

DRACULA
THE DEAD TRAVEL FAST

BY ANDY FISH

SPECIAL THANKS TO JIM RIEL AND VERONICA FISH

ALTHOUGH IT SEEMS THERE CAN BE LITTLE CHANCE OF IT BEING TRUE, HE INSISTS THAT IT IS.
REGARDLESS, IT SHOULD GIVE YOU A LOOK INTO HIS STATE OF MIND.
I'M ENCLOSING A JOURNAL HE HAS SAID HE KEPT FOR YOUR PERUSAL.
I LEAVE IT TO YOU TO DRAW YOUR OWN CONCLUSIONS, BUT I WANT YOU TO KNOW HE HAS MADE QUITE THE IMPRESSION ON US ALL.
HIS SOFT CHARM AND KIND DEMEANOR HAVE WON OUR HEARTS. HE HAS SUCH A GOOD AND GENTLE SOUL.
Jon HARKER
WE LOOK FORWARD TO MEETING YOU WHEN YOU MAKE THE LONG TRIP FROM ENGLAND. YOURS VERY TRULY, SISTER AGATHA

JON HARKER'S JOURNAL...
MAY 3, 1897
My name is Jonathan Harker, and I am recording in my journal events on my meeting with my client, Count Dracula. Traveling through strange lands I am clearly regarded as an outsider.
The train into Buda Pesth ran several minutes late, but I was fortunate that the carriage for Bistritz waited for me.
Judging by the speed at which we traveled down roads of ill repair the driver intended to make up for any lost time. I feared for the well-being of his poor horse.
My committment to keeping a travel journal occupies my time, although the growing darkness makes it increasingly difficult to write.
My fellow travelers warned me of strange dangers in the area, in very broken English.

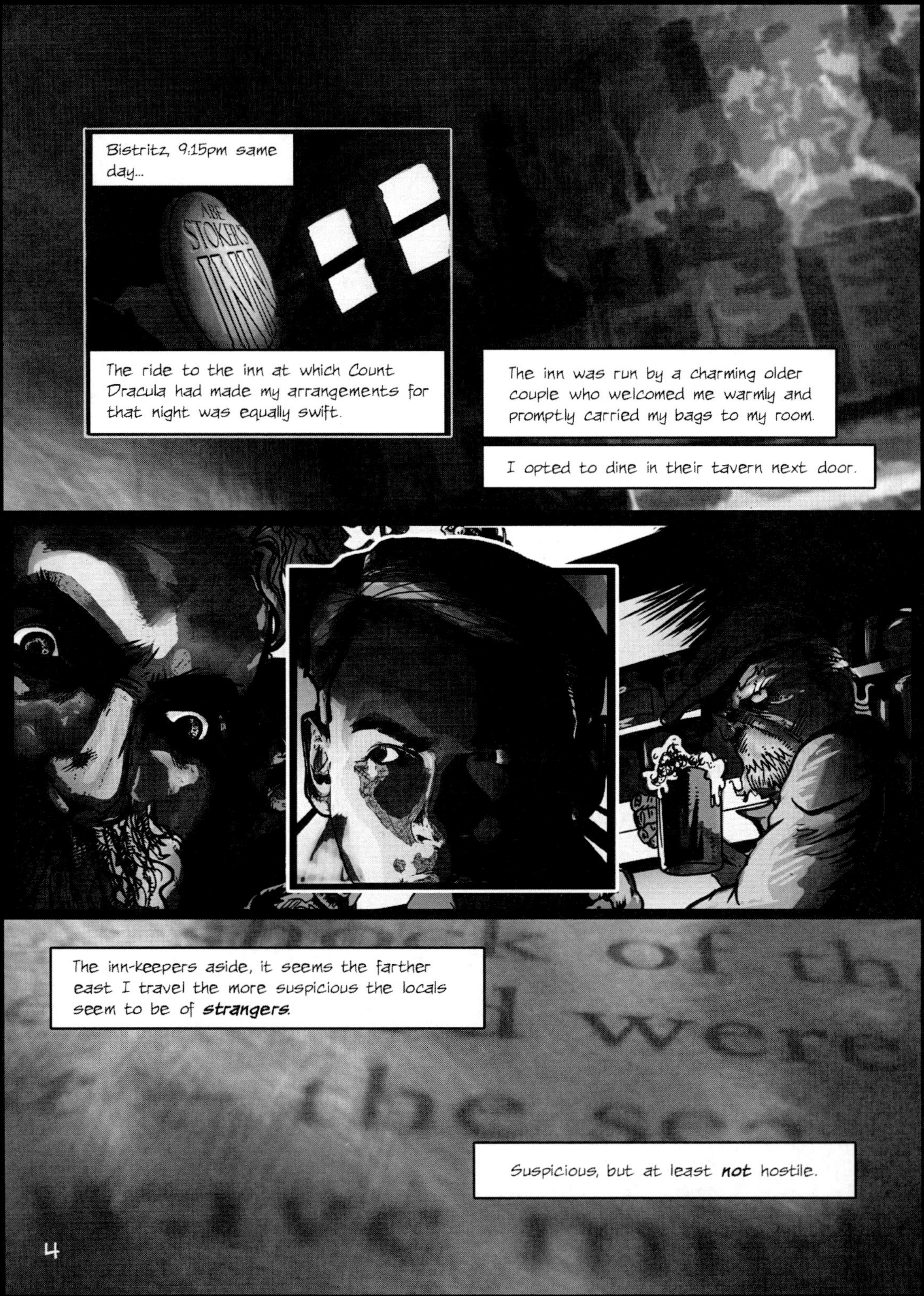
Bistritz, 9:15pm same day...
ABE STOKER'S INN
The ride to the inn at which Count Dracula had made my arrangements for that night was equally swift.
The inn was run by a charming older couple who welcomed me warmly and promptly carried my bags to my room.
I opted to dine in their tavern next door.
The inn-keepers aside, it seems the farther east I travel the more suspicious the locals seem to be of **strangers**.
Suspicious, but at least **not** hostile.

Well...
Not yet anyway.
Best to eat a hot meal and then *retire*.
MY, ISN'T THAT... IT SMELLS SO... UM...
THANK YOU. THANK YOU VERY MUCH.

HERR ENGLISHMAN?
YES?
MUST YOU GO? MUST YOU?
DO YOU KNOW WHAT THE DAY IS TOMORROW?
UM, MAY THE FOURTH?
YES. BUT DO YOU KNOW WHAT THE DAY IS?
IT IS THE EVE OF SAINT GEORGE'S DAY. THE DAY THAT EVIL THINGS HAVE FULL SWAY IN THE WORLD.
YOU ARE GOING TO THE BORGO PASS TOMORROW TO MEET YOUR RIDE. I IMPLORE YOU NOT TO GO.
"TONIGHT EVIL SPIRITS, WAMPYRES AND THE UNDEAD WILL RISE AND STALK THE LIVING. YOU WILL NOT BE SAFE OUT THERE."
MADAME, YOUR CONCERN IS CERTAINLY APPRECIATED, BUT I AM ON BUSINESS TO MEET A VERY IMPORTANT CLIENT.
I'M AFRAID SATAN HIMSELF COULDN'T STOP ME.
IF YOU'LL JUST SHOW ME TO MY ROOM?
THEN TAKE THIS AND WEAR IT ALWAYS...
...PLEASE, FOR YOUR MOTHER'S SAKE.

My bed was comfortable enough, but I could not sleep. My mouth was dry. Too much paprika at dinner perhaps? Nerves?
The old woman's talk of the supernatural surely didn't help. In the morning she handed me a note she had forgotten to give me when I first arrived, written by Dracula:
"MY FRIEND. WELCOME TO THE CARPATHIANS. I AM ANXIOUSLY EXPECTING YOU. SLEEP WELL TONIGHT. AT THREE TOMORROW THE DILIGENCE WILL START FOR BUKOVINA; A PLACE ON IT IS KEPT FOR YOU. AT THE BORGO PASS MY CARRIAGE WILL AWAIT YOU AND WILL BRING YOU TO ME.
I TRUST THAT YOUR JOURNEY FROM LONDON HAS BEEN A HAPPY ONE, AND THAT YOU WILL ENJOY YOUR STAY IN MY BEAUTIFUL LAND.
YOUR FRIEND, -D."
At dawn I gave up on sleep and went to town.
I had promised Mina I would bring her back a trinket or souvenir authentic to the region.
Mina is truly a very modern woman, well prepared for the coming Century.
She is as curious as any man, studying business and world customs. Someday we'll travel.
It seems that every superstition in the world is gathered into the horseshoe of the Carpathians.
The carriage assigned to take me to meet the Count's was scheduled at 3pm so I hurried back to the Inn after lunch.

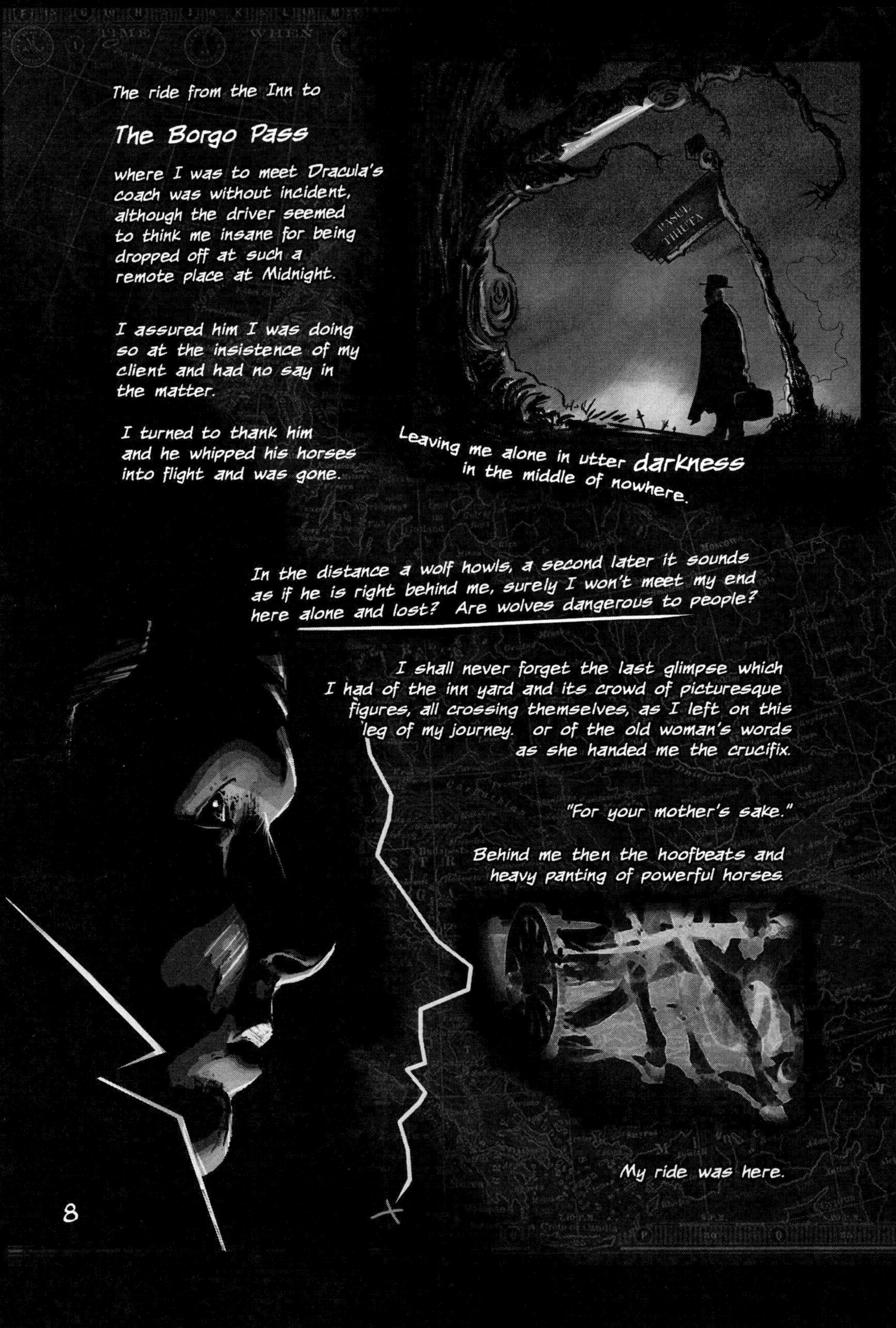
The ride from the Inn to
The Borgo Pass
where I was to meet Dracula's coach was without incident, although the driver seemed to think me insane for being dropped off at such a remote place at Midnight.
I assured him I was doing so at the insistence of my client and had no say in the matter.
I turned to thank him and he whipped his horses into flight and was gone.
PASUL TIHUTA
Leaving me alone in utter darkness in the middle of nowhere.
In the distance a wolf howls, a second later it sounds as if he is right behind me, surely I won't meet my end here alone and lost? Are wolves dangerous to people?
I shall never forget the last glimpse which I had of the inn yard and its crowd of picturesque figures, all crossing themselves, as I left on this leg of my journey. or of the old woman's words as she handed me the crucifix.
"For your mother's sake."
Behind me then the hoofbeats and heavy panting of powerful horses.
My ride was here.

The horses stopped short.
He had arrived with impossible speed and stealth. Steam seemed to rise from his steed.
The line from Burger's 'Leonore' came to mind.
"Denn die Todten Reiten Schnell."
"For the Dead travel fast."
ARE YOU THE COACHMAN FROM CASTLE DRACULA?
AYE.
THE NIGHT AIR IS CHILL, MEINE HERR
MY MASTER THE COUNT BADE ME TAKE ALL CARE OF YOU.
COME, ON OUR WAY WE MUST BE.

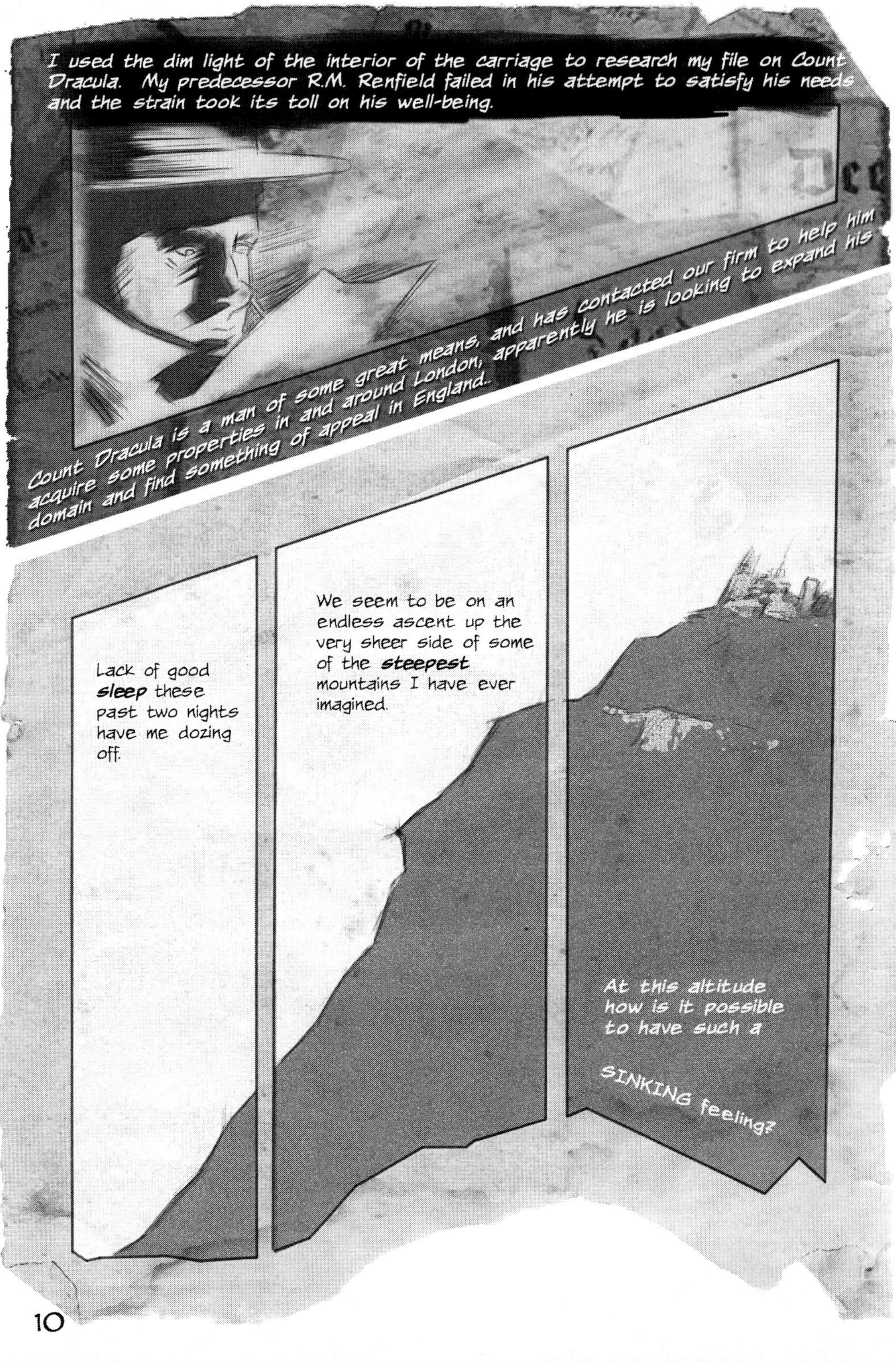

I used the dim light of the interior of the carriage to research my file on Count Dracula. My predecessor R.M. Renfield failed in his attempt to satisfy his needs and the strain took its toll on his well-being.
Count Dracula is a man of some great means, and has contacted our firm to help him acquire some properties in and around London, apparently he is looking to expand his domain and find something of appeal in England.
Lack of good sleep these past two nights have me dozing off.
We seem to be on an endless ascent up the very sheer side of some of the steepest mountains I have ever imagined.
At this altitude how is it possible to have such a
SINKING feeling?

Giant WOLVES soon surrounded us as if to provide some manner of escort. The Pack grew larger and frenzied.
Much to my alarm the driver halted the carriage and STEPPED OUT among them. As he raised a hand, the WOLVES stopped on command.
He glanced my way and smiled as he climbed back into the driver's seat.
CASTLE DRACULA
We entered the main gates and stopped. Both my bags and the DRIVER had disappeared.

Before me stood a huge wooden door.
KNOCK KNOCK!
HELLO?

KA-TA CHING!
KA-TA CHENG!
KA DOOM!
KA-TA CHING!

Count DRACULA

A MONTH? THAT'S **NOT** POSSIBLE!
YOU WILL STAY WITH ME... ***ONE MONTH!***
MY ENGLISH IS POOR, AND YOU WILL CORRECT ANY OF MY MISTAKES.
IT MUST BE AS PERFECT AS YOURS. YOU WILL INSTRUCT ME, AND BE ***QUITE*** HARSH.
ONE MONTH, MISTER HARKER.
COME, THE NIGHT AIR IS CHILL AND YOU MUST NEED TO ***EAT*** AND ***REST.***
IT IS LATE AND MY SERVANTS HAVE RETIRED. I SHALL SEE TO YOUR COMFORT MYSELF.
I THINK YOUR ENGLISH IS ***QUITE GOOD,*** COUNT.
COME...

I PRAY YOU, BE SEATED AND SUP HOW YOU PLEASE. YOU WILL, I TRUST, EXCUSE ME THAT I DO NOT JOIN YOU.
I HAVE DINED ALREADY, AND I DO NOT SUP.
GOOD HEAVENS COUNT, THIS IS QUITE AMAZING!
TRULY A FEAST!
MY EMPLOYER P.J. HAWKINS SENDS HIS MOST SINCERE REGARDS AND REGRETS THAT HE COULD NOT JOIN US.
HE SUFFERS AN ATTACK OF THE GOUT.
BUT HE HAS INSTRUCTED ME TO SEE TO ALL OF YOUR NEEDS.
MISTER HARKER.
TRANSYLVANIA HAS BECOME A DRY AND THIRSTY LAND,
NOT YOUNG AND FULL OF BLOOD LIKE YOUR OWN ENGLAND.
I WANT TO LEARN OF ENGLAND.

I DON'T KNOW IF IT'S THE HOT FOOD OR THE COUNT'S HOSPITALITY BUT ALL MY NERVOUS MISGIVINGS JUST MELT AWAY AND I RELAX.
THE PAPERWORK SEEMS IN ORDER.
TELL ME OF THIS HOUSE YOU HAVE FOUND FOR ME IN ENGLAND.
TELL ME OF ENGLAND, MR HARKER.
WELL, THE ESTATE IS CALLED CARFAX, NEARLY 400 ACRES.
IT IS RATHER MEDIEVAL AND VERY PRIVATE.
BORDERED BY A LARGE STONE WALL ON ONE SIDE AND A PRIVATE ASYLUM ON THE OTHER.
THIS SATAY IS DELICIOUS, COUNT. AS IS THE WINE.
MIGHT I POUR YOU A GLASS?
I NEVER DRINK...
...WINE...
...MISTER HARKER.
DEED

REGISTRY of D E E D
I TRUST EVERYTHING IS TO YOUR SATISFACTION, COUNT?
QUIET, MISTER HARKER!
LISTEN TO THEM! THE CHILDREN OF THE NIGHT...
In the distance we could hear the growing howl of wolves.
...WHAT MUSIC THEY MAKE!

7 May-
I slept late and found a note from the Count saying he would be out for most of the day.
I explored the Castle and to my delight I found an impressive Library of English Literature.
The Count must have assembled such a collection
in his efforts to learn English!
One thing is certain...
I wouldn't starve for reading material.
MISTER HARKER! I AM GLAD YOU FOUND YOUR WAY HERE, FOR I AM SURE THERE IS MUCH THAT WILL INTEREST YOU.
YOU MAY GO ANYWHERE IN THE CASTLE, EXCEPT WHERE THE DOORS ARE LOCKED, WHERE YOU WILL NOT WISH TO GO.
TRANSYLVANIA IS NOT ENGLAND.
OUR WAYS ARE NOT YOUR WAYS, AND THERE SHALL BE TO YOU MANY STRANGE THINGS.

The Count kept me up until nearly dawn telling him stories of England and of the properties he'd acquired. I was only really familiar with Carfax Abbey as it sits very near the grounds of Mina's dear friend Lucy Westenra's family home.
Sleep denied me, and what little of it I got was filled with nightmares.
The **Count** is right. Transylvania is **not** England. It is a strange otherworldly place born more of madness than man.

GOOD MORNING.
The entire room was visible to me in the reflection of my shaving mirror...
...yet here was the Count, standing behind me,
With no reflection even as he drew closer!
TAKE CARE HOW YOU CUT YOURSELF...

...IT IS MORE DANGEROUS THAN YOU THINK!
THE BLOOD, MISTER HARKER...
THE BLOOD IS THE LIFE!
The sight of the old woman's Crucifix repelled his advances.
ECH!

Mina Murray's Journal; May 22. We arrive a few minutes ahead of schedule, and I'm excited to see my dear friend Lucy.
WHITBY
The poor thing is fighting off several suitors (Lucy has always been popular with boys),
and it shall be nice to take a break from my studies while I wait to hear from Jonathan.
The joy of travel has often eluded me. I fear I'll be lost forever, never finding Lucy, or my bags.
EXCUSE ME, PLEASE. YES, PARDON ME. EXCUSE ME.
Everyone seems to know where they're going...
...except me.
I don't know what's wrong with me. I'm overwhelmed by the crowds. Suddenly I have a terrible feeling of dread, a horrible premonition.
MINA!
Mina MURRAY
Has something happened to Jon?
Oh thank heavens!

LUCY I WAS SO WORRIED I WOULDN'T BE ABLE TO...
MINA! OH HEAVENS *THERE* YOU ARE!
YOU LOOK WONDERFUL! OH MINA, LET ME INTRODUCE MY DEAR, *DEAR* FRIEND...
Lucy WESTENRA
Quincey MORRIS
HOWDY MA'AM. I'M RIGHT PLEASED TO MEET YOU.
OF COURSE, THE COWBOY FROM AMERICA! I'VE HEARD ALL ABOUT YOU SIR!
I'M NOT SURE IF I SHOULD BE *FLATTERED* OR *HORRIFIED.*
FEAR *NOT*, MR. MORRIS.
I ASSURE YOU IT WAS ALL *VERY FLATTERING.*
WELL I'M THANKFUL FOR THAT!
OKAY YOU TWO, THAT'S ENOUGH GOSSIP. LET'S GET MINA HOME, SHE MUST BE FAMISHED!
MOTHER IS HAVING ONE OF HER COCKTAIL PARTIES TONIGHT MINA, YOU'RE JUST IN TIME!

...WRETCHED THING.
A FOUL BAUBLE OF MAN'S OWN VANITY.
KA-RINK!
AWAY WITH IT.
BEWARE MISTER HARKER.
BEWARE PLACING YOUR FAITH ...
IN FALSE TRINKETS.

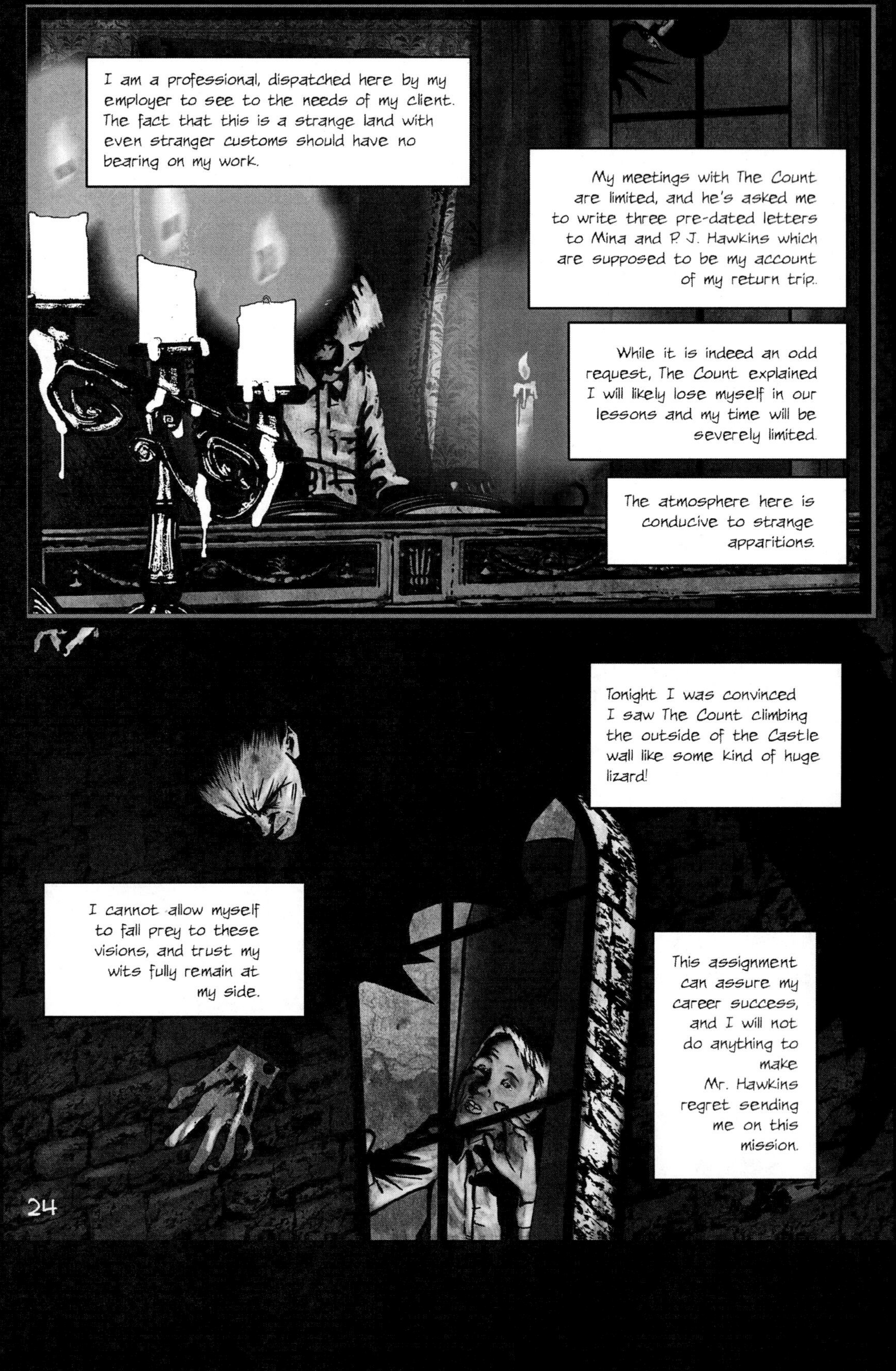
I am a professional, dispatched here by my employer to see to the needs of my client. The fact that this is a strange land with even stranger customs should have no bearing on my work.
My meetings with The Count are limited, and he's asked me to write three pre-dated letters to Mina and P. J. Hawkins which are supposed to be my account of my return trip.
While it is indeed an odd request, The Count explained I will likely lose myself in our lessons and my time will be severely limited.
The atmosphere here is conducive to strange apparitions.
Tonight I was convinced I saw The Count climbing the outside of the Castle wall like some kind of huge lizard!
I cannot allow myself to fall prey to these visions, and trust my wits fully remain at my side.
This assignment can assure my career success, and I will not do anything to make Mr. Hawkins regret sending me on this mission.

OUTSIDE LONDON.
DR. SEWARD'S JOURNAL; MAY 4, 1897
NO IMPROVEMENT IN APPETITE TODAY. I CANNOT EAT OR SLEEP SINCE MY LUCY REBUFFED MY PROPOSAL DAYS AGO.
I AM OVERWHELMED BY A FEELING OF MOURNING, NOTHING SEEMS OF SUFFICIENT IMPORTANCE TO ME.
I'VE THROWN MYSELF INTO MY WORK, CHOOSING A PATIENT WHO HAS AFFORDED ME MUCH INTEREST— R.M. RENFIELD, 51. GREAT PHYSICAL STRENGTH, PERIODS OF GLOOM FOLLOWED BY EUPHORIA.
EXTREMELY DANGEROUS BOTH TO HIMSELF AND TO OTHERS.
BROUGHT HERE AFTER A TRIP ABROAD, WHERE HIS WORK AS A SOLICITOR BROUGHT HIM TO...
...LUCY.
GUARD, UNLOCK MR. RENFIELD'S ROOM AND WAIT IN THE HALL.
YES DOCTOR SEWARD.
SO TIRED.
I SLEPT NOT A WHIT LAST NIGHT, AND I FEAR I'M IN FOR MORE OF THE SAME.
I KNOW IT'S SOMEONE ELSE, IT HAS TO BE, AND MY THOUGHTS HAVE TURNED TO OBSESSION SINCE SHE WON'T TELL ME WHO.
Jack SEWARD
GOOD DAY MR. RENFIELD. HOW ARE WE TODAY?
DAMN IT, I'M A PROFESSIONAL MAN. CAN I BE THIS DISTRAUGHT OVER THE LOSS OF A WOMAN?

"DAY"? DOCTOR SEWARD? IT'S NOT DAY— IT'S ***NIGHT!*** I CAN SEE ***THE MOON*** THROUGH MY WINDOW.
SO VERY NICE TO SEE YOU!
WON'T YOU COME IN?
R.M. RENFIELD

DR SEWARD'S JOURNAL
SUBJECT R.M. RENFIELD'S CASE CONTINUES TO FASCINATE ME.
SINCE HE'S MAKING PROG-RESS WE ARE ALLOWING HIM TIME OUT OF HIS RESTRAINTS.
HE HAS TAKEN TO RAISING INSECTS IN A QUASI FARM ENVIRONMENT HE'S BUILT IN HIS CELL.
PREVIOUSLY HE HAD ASKED ME FOR A KITTEN, I ASSUMED FOR COMPANIONSHIP.
LITTLE BUG...LITTLE BUG...
...LITTLE BLOOD...
...THE BLOOD...
I THOUGHT AT FIRST THAT THE INSECTS WERE A SUBSTITUTE FOR A PET.
THAT DOES NOT APPEAR TO BE THE CASE.
CHOMP!
...IS THE LIFE!

TRANSYLVANIA
I struggled to keep my senses as I watched the Count slither down and out of the castle.
Knowing he was gone, I decided to search the maze-like hallways of his house.
I had been told not to enter certain rooms.
That night I found out why.
This first room, now unlocked, was a bedroom?!
It wasn't the Count's room, which was directly below mine. Was there another guest?
And why was I forbidden to enter?

Delirium or dream I can't be certain, but suddenly I was no longer alone in the room.
GO ON. YOU ARE FIRST. YOURS IS THE RIGHT TO BEGIN
HE IS YOUNG AND STRONG.
ENOUGH FOR ALL OF US!

STRONG.
FULL OF LIFE.
FULL-BLOODED.
STOP!

HOW DARE YOU TOUCH HIM!
ANY OF YOU!
HOW DARE YOU CAST EYES ON HIM WHEN I HAVE FORBIDDEN IT!?
ARE WE TO HAVE NOTHING TONIGHT THEN?
NO.
YOU WILL FEED.
GGEEEGGEEYYHHHAHHAWWWAAA!!

PLEASE, COUNT...
I WANT TO GO HOME.
My wits cracked as I watched them feed on the infant.
NOT ONE MINUTE WILL YOU STAY IN MY HOUSE AGAINST YOUR WILL.
NOT ONE MINUTE.
I TRUST YOU ARE PACKED?
OF COURSE, THERE IS THE MATTER OF MY COACH, IT IS AWAY UNTIL THE MORN.
WHEN IT RETURNS I WILL ARRANGE FOR IT TO RETURN YOU TO THE VILLAGE.
I AM SORRY THAT I HAVE BEEN A POOR HOST.
PLEASE!
LET ME GO NOW!
I'LL WALK!

I'LL WALK!!
YES MISTER HARKER.
I opened my eyes to find myself fully dressed and in the Castle foyer.
It was like a mad dream.
I HEARD YOU.
I wanted to leave, I wanted to go home, to go to...
Mina.

DEAR GOD.
TAKE CARE MY YOUNG FRIEND.
TAKE CARE ON YOUR JOURNEY.
THE WOODS AT NIGHT CAN BE FULL OF DANGER.
TRANSYLVANIA IS NOT YOUR ENGLAND.

MISTER HARKER?
DO YOU NEED HELP WITH YOUR BAG?
NO!
PLEASE!
CLOSE THE DOOR! PLEASE!
PLEASE!

I didn't leave, of course, nor was the coach at my disposal the next morning.
Days passed and I devised a clever plan.
I would bribe the Gypsies to deliver a coded note to *Mina* in England.
I was certain they would abandon their loyalty to Dracula if I *paid* enough.
I struggled to get their *attention.*
Confident in my plan which would surely bring help,
KA-SHINK!
I packed my bags so I'd be ready to go.
Hours later the *Count* came in and tossed my note on the bed.
The Gypsies had brought him my bag.
No bribe could overcome their loyalty or fear.

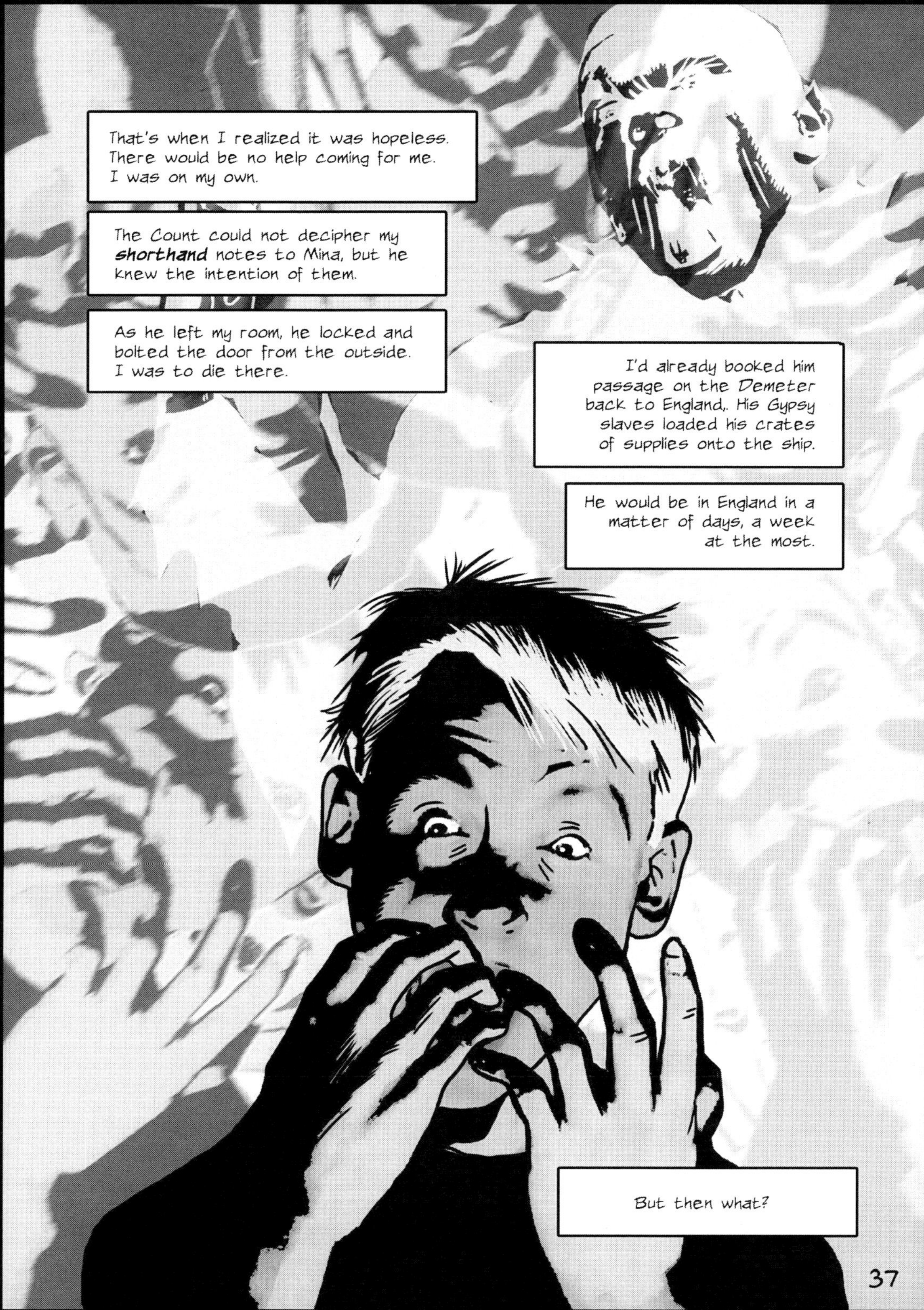
That's when I realized it was hopeless. There would be no help coming for me. I was on my own.
The Count could not decipher my **shorthand** notes to Mina, but he knew the intention of them.
As he left my room, he locked and bolted the door from the outside. I was to die there.
I'd already booked him passage on the *Demeter* back to England,. His Gypsy slaves loaded his crates of supplies onto the ship.
He would be in England in a matter of days, a week at the most.
But then what?

What could this **Monster** want with England?
Of course!
How could I have been so blind?
The Count's own words came back to me.
"Transylvania is a dry and thirsty land..."
HAAAAAAIIIIIIIIEEEEEEEEEEEEEEEEEEEEE!!!!
He needs England...
...to ***feed.***

"...a dry and thirsty land..."
"Not full of blood like your own England."
Whispers from the hallway.
TONIGHT, TONIGHT HE IS OURS.
TONIGHT WE FEED.
I wasn't alone.
I barricaded my door, as **effective** as hiding under the **bedspread**.
Which was my **next** plan.
I'LL JUST STAY HERE. RIGHT HERE.
YES,
STAY HERE UNTIL..
...UNTIL...
...LIKE HELL I WILL.
I'd had enough of being a victim.

MINA'S JOURNAL. Lucy's dinner party in Whitby.
I'M SORRY ARTHUR HAD TO LEAVE. DID YOU REALLY LIKE HIM?
HE'S WONDERFUL, LUCY, REALLY. IT'S JUST SEEING YOUR BEAU MAKES ME WORRY...
...ABOUT JON. I'VE NOT HEARD FROM HIM.
I'D BE CONCERNED. RENFIELD CAME BACK FROM TRANSYLVANIA A RAVING LOON.
JACK!
I'M SORRY TO BE SO BLUNT, LUCY.
I'M SURE HIS TRAGIC TURN HAD NOTHING TO DO WITH HIS ASSIGNMENT.
JON IS PROBABLY BUSY WITH—
HAVE YOU BEEN DRINKING? THERE IS SUCH A THING AS TACT.
AS WELL AS PATIENT CONFIDENTIALITY AND TRUST.
MINA YOU SHOULD GO AND ASK MR. HAWKINS ABOUT RENFIELD.
DOCTOR—PATIENT RELATIONSHIPS SHOULD BE—
SACRED?
SACRED?
WAS THAT WHAT YOU WERE GOING TO SAY, LUCY?
LIKE A PROMISE TO WED?
OH JACK, ARE WE GOING TO START THIS AGAIN?
BUSY WITH CLIENTS AND PAPER WORK.
I'M SURE JON'S FINE.
I SHOULD GO, QUINCEY IS...
I FAIL TO SEE HOW IT'S ANY DIFFERENT, LUCY.
JACK, THIS IS NEITHER THE TIME OR PLACE—
WELL I GUESS I'LL LEAVE YOU TWO TO CATCH UP.

MISTER RENFIELD?
A TRAGIC CASE.
HIS WORKLOAD BECAME TOO MUCH FOR HIM.
I BLAME MYSELF.
I GUESS I'M CONCERNED BECAUSE I'VE NOT HEARD FROM JONATHAN.
JONATHAN? THERE IS NO CONNECTION MY DEAR.
JON IS A GENTLE SOUL, BUT STRONG-WILLED.
IS THERE SOMETHING ELSE WRONG, MINA?
WHAT?
NO.
IT'S JUST BEEN NEARLY A MONTH.
COUNT DRACULA IS AN IMPORTANT CLIENT, CERTAINLY TAKING UP ALL OF HIS FREE TIME.
I'M SURE THE REMOTENESS OF TRANSYLVANIA ALSO HAMPERS HIS COMMUNICATION.
THANK YOU FOR COMING BY, MINA.
YOU TOO, MR. MORRIS.
YOU SURE YOU WON'T STAY FOR MORE TEA?
NO, THANK YOU. IT WAS WONDERFUL.
I'M CERTAIN WE'LL HEAR FROM JON VERY SOON.
YES OF COURSE.
THANK YOU, MISTER HAWKINS.
41

TRANSYLVANIA
The Gypsies work tirelessly in the courtyard, loading one heavy crate after another onto horse-drawn carriages.
As for me, attempting to escape these woods during the day would be danger-ous, but going at night was suicide.
But I had no choice.
The Count had promised me to his vampire wives on the night they devoured that small child.
Their dinner wouldn't be waiting for them.

The door to my room was locked, but the window wasn't.
I needed only to navigate a tiny ledge some 300 feet up to make it to one of The Count's many rooms.
That would surely not be locked and I can make my way down from there.
I started, ever cautious, but a disturbance far below nearly caused me to fall.
BAM! BAM! BAM!
AAAAAIIIIIIIIIIEEEEEEE!!!!!!!!
?
MONSTRU!
BAM! BAM! BAM!
BAM! BAM! BAM!
MONSTRU! MI-ATI UAT EL COPIL!!
STRIGA!
ADEMENI!!
BAM! BAM! BAM!

STRIGA!
ADEMENI!!
BAM! BAM! BAM!
Although I could not understand her, from her hysterical tone I knew her to be the mother of that poor infant.
MONSTRU!
BAM! BAM! BAM!
"MONSTRU!" MI-ATI UAT EL COPIL!!
"MONSTRU!"
From my perch high above I could hear the rising growl of wolves. Before I could warn her, she heard them too.
AAAAAIIIIIIIIIIIEEEEEEEE!!!!!!!!!!
She raised her fists and stood ready to fight.

Just a few of these could be of great help on my journey.
I filled my bag— payment from the Count for services rendered.

It wasn't greed, it was necessity. I might have to bribe my way back to the village.

His wealth explained how The Count had allies in this region, despite his occasional snacking on its chidlren.

Hidden in the corner of the room was a staircase which...
SHINK!
CHUNKTZ!
SHINK!
CHUNKTZ!
MES OTT AMIT OTT!
SHINK!
...led to a cavern under the Castle.
More Gypsies bringing crates upstairs.
They seem to be filling the crates...
...with dirt? All that gold upstairs and they fill the crates with dirt?
MEGJELENÉS AMIT LÁMPA — EGY EMBER OTT!!
ÁLLÍTSA MEG OTT!
It made no sense.

A FELÜLKEREKEDIK AKARAT VOLNA -UNK ÉL HA MENEKÜLÉS!! LI NEKI HALOTT!
My presence appeared to be unwelcome.
BLAM! SPAK! BLAM! SPAK!
BLAM! S-PLING!
P-TWANG!
SON OF A BITCH!
I was a sitting duck, I had to do something.
I grabbed a nearby shovel and tried to knock the gun out of his hand.
P-TWANG!
I got it on the second try.

LESZ CSINAL EGY IZLETES ELVEZET RESZERE A FELOL-KEREKEOIK
BLAM
BLAM
SPAK!
SPBLUG!
God help me, I had no other choice.
THUD

God help me.
why?
Why would they want to kill me?
What are they protecting?
Surely not to defend these boxes of dirt.
What value can boxes of earth possibly hold?
Literally thousands of pounds in gold just upstairs, and they defend this dirt with their lives?
My god!
The Count lay in some kind of catatonic state, somewhere between sleep and death.
Lying in the very dirt itself.
What manner of monster was he? What unearthly creature now was threatening London?
Whether I lived or died no longer mattered to me...

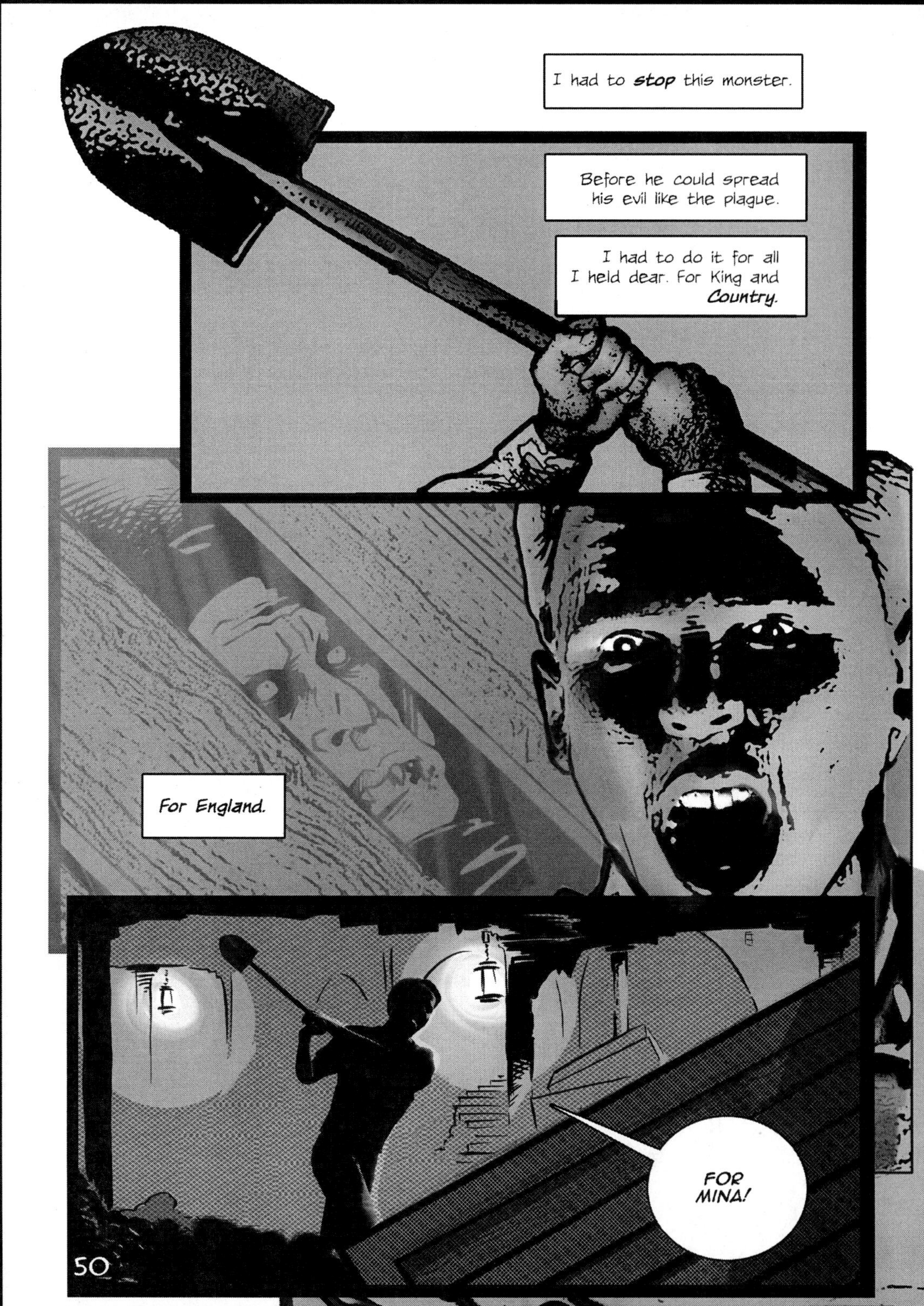
I had to stop this monster.
Before he could spread his evil like the plague.
I had to do it for all I held dear. For King and Country.
For England.
FOR MINA!

HARKER!

YOU DARE?
IMPETUOUS BOY! A MOUSE AGAINST THE LION!
I WHO HAVE LIVED A HUNDRED LIFETIMES.
DEFEATED KHAN AND HIS INVADING HORDES.
m...m...m...
min...min...mina...
I have failed, forgive me.

CAPTAIN OF THE DEMETER'S LOG
18 JUL, 1897
WE SET SAIL 6 JUL TO CALM SEA, SEASONED CREW, FIVE HANDS, TWO MATES, COOK AND MYSELF.
AS CAPTAIN I AM WRITING DOWN EVENTS IN JOURNAL AS BEST I CAN REMEMBER THEM.
THIS HAS BECOME A VOYAGE OF HELL.
GOD HELP AN OLD SAILOR TO GO HOME AGAIN.
Crew has sailed with me many times in past, with no troubles. This time events from the beginning should have given me warning but I was afraid to see them.
Cook was first to notice trouble.
I HEAR CREW, THEY THINK MY ENGRISH NOT GOOD, BUT I HEAR.
CREW SCARED. THEY SAY SOMETHING WRONG.
SUPERSTITION. MINDLESS SUPERSTITION. I'VE SEEN EVEN THE ABLEST OF HANDS SUCCUMB.
NO.
NO CAPTAIN, DIS IS NOT SAME TING.
DIS REAL FEAR.

WE ARE BARELY UNDERWAY WHEN WE ARE STOPPED AND BOARDED BY TURKISH CUSTOMS AGENTS.
THEY CLAIM ROUTINE INSPECTION, BUT THEY BEHAVE IN A VERY STRANGE MANNER AND SPEAK TO EACH OTHER IN HUSHED TONES.
INSPECTION IS VERY THOROUGH AND TIME-CONSUMING, BUT IT IS WITHOUT INCIDENT.
THEY SEEM TO BE LOOKING FOR SOMETHING, BUT THEY NEVER SAY WHAT.
THEY APPEARED TO SHARE THE SAME UNEASE AS THE CREW, AND THERE IS A PART OF ME THAT HOPED THEY WOULD FIND *SOMETHING* AND FORCE US TO TURN BACK.

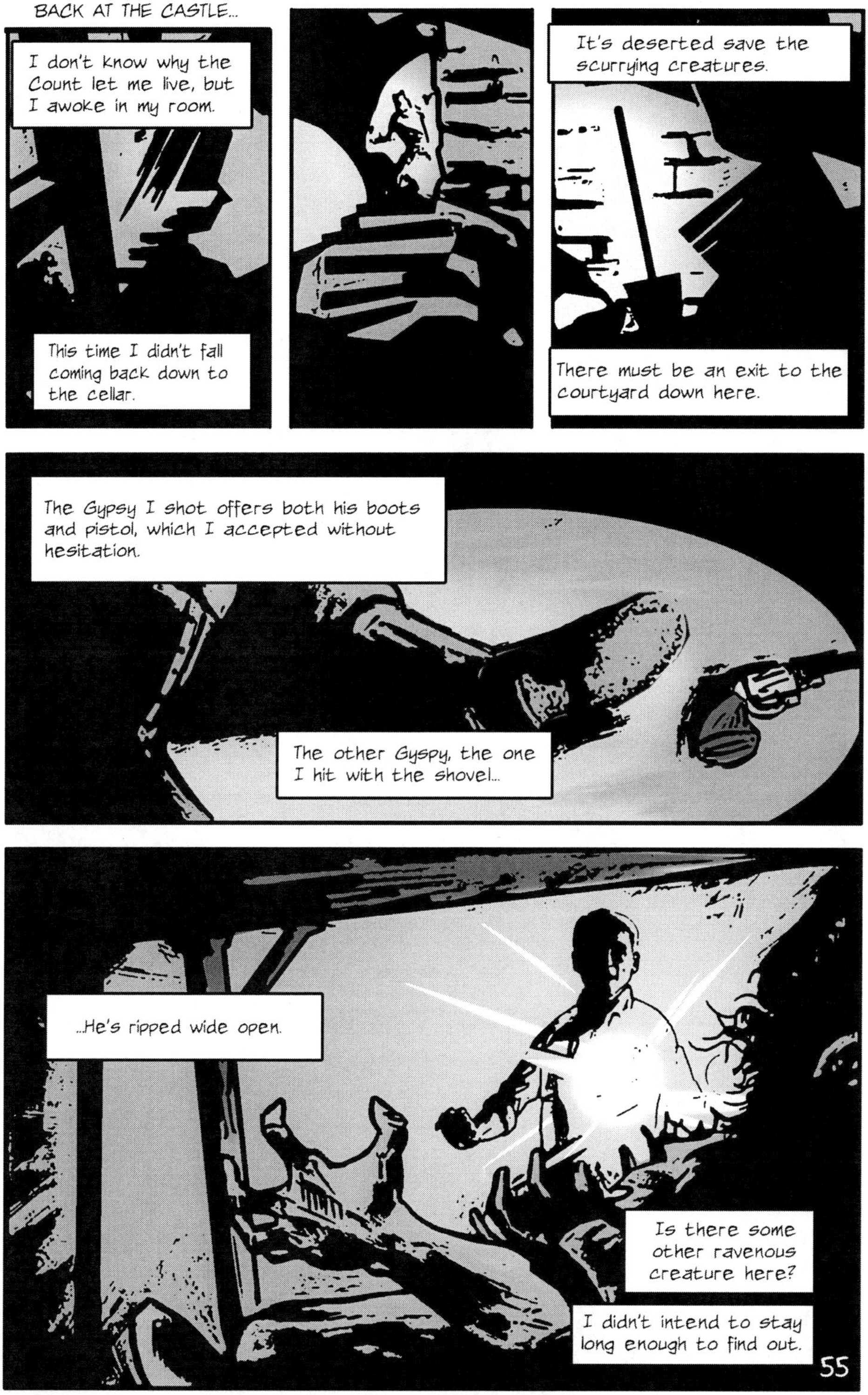
BACK AT THE CASTLE...
I don't know why the Count let me live, but I awoke in my room.
This time I didn't fall coming back down to the cellar.
It's deserted save the scurrying creatures.
There must be an exit to the courtyard down here.
The Gypsy I shot offers both his boots and pistol, which I accepted without hesitation.
The other Gyspy, the one I hit with the shovel...
...He's ripped wide open.
Is there some other ravenous creature here?
I didn't intend to stay long enough to find out.
55

I made it through the courtyard and out of the Castle, running full clip down the main road without incident.
It was so easy, far too easy.
But not for long.
I dared not turn, but I knew they were there. Right **behind** me.

I was raised a proper English gentleman. The finest prep schools, University.
HF!
I'd gotten into a boyhood scrap once, more a slap-fest: my mate had taken my lunch.
He'd grown up in a London slum, fighting through every day.
He'd learned the meaning of survival.
He trounced me, but we eventually became friends. He called me "Good Ol' Harker."
Turn the other cheek, run from a fight, talk my way out of trouble.
I envied my mate's ability to fight.
I admired him.
Now more than ever.
OKAY.
LET'S DO THIS.
I really said that out loud.

I was ready to fight, ready to stand my ground. I saw something in their eyes...
...*Fear.*
The third one, the biggest, showed no sign of fear and lunged at me.
It was massive, easily my size; this was no normal wolf.
I **fought** back. I **might** have screamed a bit, but I fought back.

THE DEMETER...
AHOY?
SOMEONE THERE?
PETROFSKY?
IS THAT YOU?
THUMP!

KAPITAN!!!
DEAR GOD PETROFSKY WHAT IS IT?
IT'S VARTAN! I WENT TO RELIEVE HIM ON WATCH AND, AND...
HE'S GONE!
"GONE?"
FALLEN OVERBOARD?
NO SIR! I HEARD HIM SCREAM! SOMETHING WAS ATTACKING HIM BUT BY THE TIME I GOT THERE HE WAS GONE!
I SAW HIM DO IT.
PETROFSKY IS A FINE SAILOR, NOT PRONE TO PANIC, BUT THIS OVERWHELMING FEAR MUST BE STOPPED BEFORE IT SPREADS THROUGH THE CREW.

WE HAVE SEARCHED THE SHIP TOP TO BOTTOM, HE'S GONE.
VARTAN MUST HAVE FALLEN OVERBOARD DURING WATCH LAST NIGHT.
PETROFSKY SAID HE HEARD HIM CRY FOR HELP!
YES HE WOULD HAVE CALLED FOR HELP IF HE FELL OVER.
HE WAS ATTACKED.
PETROFSKY IS DELIRIOUS IN SICKBAY NOW.
WE'VE NOT SEARCHED BOXES IN HOLD.
SOMETHING IS ON BOARD. WE NEED TO SEARCH THE WHOLE SHIP.
THOSE "BOXES" ARE CARGO...
...CARGO WE'VE BEEN HIRED TO DELIVER TO ENGLAND.
DO YOU WANT TO EXPLAIN TO COUNT DRACULA WHY WE SEARCHED HIS PROPERTY?
WE NEED TO SEARCH THIS WHOLE SHIP.
61

THE CREW SEARCHED EACH AND EVERY BOX, CONVINCED THAT THERE WAS SOME CREATURE HIDING INSIDE.
THE MATE CHASTISED THEM FOR GIVING IN TO HYSTERIA.
WITH EACH NEW BOX OPENED, THE SCENT OF DECAYING EARTH BEGAN TO FILL THE SHIP'S HOLD.
BOX TWENTY DID REVEAL A STOWAWAY, BUT NOT OF THE DEMONIC PERSUASION.
THE SCREAM OF THE CREWMAN WHO DISCOVERED IT MIGHT HAVE LED ONE TO THINK HE'D FOUND SATAN HIMSELF.

CAPTAIN'S LOG
JUL 18
MATE HAS WHEEL SO I MIGHT REST, BUT IT'S MORE THAN THE SEA THAT'S *UNEASY.*
SEARCH OF TWO DAYS AGO HAS CONVINCED CREW THERE IS NOTHING TO FEAR ON BOARD. THEY ARE LIKE MEN *REBORN.*
STORMY SEAS KEEP ALL HANDS BUSY, TOO BUSY TO THINK OF MINDLESS *SUPERSTITION* OR *FEAR.*
THE ROCKING OF THE BOAT IS SOOTHING TO AN OLD SEA HAND. LULLING ME TO SLEEP.

NOT REALIZING WE ARE SAILING
FULLSPEED INTO HELL ITSELF.

LONDON
I'M AFRAID THAT IS QUITE *IMPOSSIBLE,* MISTER RENFIELD.
PLEASE DOCTOR SEWARD *PLEASE!!*
A KITTEN. PLEASE.
DR. SEWARD'S JOURNAL
RENFIELD'S PLEAS TO RECEIVE A PET, SOMETHING TO TAKE RESPONSIBILITY FOR, IS AN INDICATION THAT HE VALUES LIFE ITSELF, AND MAY BE MOVING AWAY FROM HIS HOMICIDAL TENDENCIES.
THERE REMAINS THE FACT THAT I OBSERVED HIM DEVOUR A BOX FULL OF SPIDERS WITH A CERTAIN ECSTASY.
I ASSURED HIM I WOULD CONSIDER HIS REQUEST AT A LATER DATE, BUT THE FOLLOWING DAY HE CAPTURED A SPARROW AND SEEMED TO HAVE IT TRAINED TO HIS WISHES.
PERHAPS WE'VE UNCOVERED RENFIELD'S REAL TALENT.

MINA'S JOURNAL
FROM OUR "FAVORITE SEAT" AT THE EDGE OF THE ESTATE WE COULD SEE A SHIP WAS CAUSING SOME EXCITEMENT IN THE HARBOR BELOW.
MISTER SWALES!
WHAT IS ALL THE COMMOTION FOR?
YOU 'AVEN'T 'EARD MISS LUCY?
IT'S IN ALL THE PAPERS.
IT'S A GHOST SHIP WHAT COME IN.
A SHIP WITH NO CREW ABOARD.
AN' A CAPTAIN AS DEAD AS A COFFIN'S NAIL.
'IS HANDS TIED TO THE VERY WHEEL OF THE SHIP!
IT'S 'ORRIBLE MA'AM!

DESPITE HAVING NO LIVING CREW THE SHIP MANAGED TO GROUND ITSELF IN THE HARBOR, AND AGAINST MY BETTER JUDGMENT WE WALKED DOWN TO SEE IT FIRSTHAND-- JUST IN TIME TO SEE A HUGE DOG LEAP FROM THE DECK AND LOSE ITSELF IN THE GROWING CROWD.
DID YOU SEE THAT!?

THE ASYLUM
I'M SO SORRY TO BOTHER YOU DR. SEWARD, BUT HE'S BEEN LIKE THIS ALL NIGHT.
WE CAN'T CALM HIM.
IT'S NO BOTHER, EVAN, I WANT TO BE NOTIFIED OF ANY CHANGES WITH THIS ONE.
MISTER RENFIELD?
HOW IS YOUR NEW PET BIRD?
HE ATE IT, SIR, AND VOMITED IT UP.
AGGHHH! AGGHHHH! YES! THE MASTER IS COMING!!
THAT'S UNFORTUNATE.
MISTER RENFIELD, IT'S DOCTOR SEWARD.
HE'S STARK RAVING MAD.
I'M HERE MASTER! I'M HERE! YES! YES! I HEAR YOU! I HEAR YOU!

MINA'S JOURNAL: I AM BY NO MEANS CLINICALLY TRAINED IN SUCH THINGS BUT LUCY'S MIND SEEMS TROUBLED, AND SHE HAS TAKEN TO SLEEPWALKING. AT FIRST I FOUND IT CHARMING.
LUCY!?
ONE NIGHT IN PARTICULAR I SAW SOMETHING TERRIFYING...
LUCY!!
MY GOD!
WHATEVER OR WHOEVER WAS THERE WAS GONE. COULD IT HAVE BEEN MY IMAGINATION?
LUCY!
LUCY! ARE YOU OKAY?
OH GOD YOU'RE FREEZING!
LET'S GET YOU INSIDE!

I KNOW THIS IS SERIOUS, QUINCEY.
MINA FOUND HER WANDERING THE ESTATE IN HER NIGHT DRESS!
NOW SHE'S RUNNING A FEVER.
IT'S BAD, I KNOW IT.
JACK'S HERE. HE'LL MAKE SURE SHE'S OK.
RIGHT JACK?
BE CALM ART.
Arthur HOLMWOOD
MY GOD SHE LOOKS LIKE AN ANGEL!
JACK!
YES, QUINCEY, OF COURSE I WILL.
I'LL LOOK AFTER HER, ARTHUR, NO NEED TO WORRY.

MINA'S JOURNAL: In the days since the incident with Lucy she's gotten considerably worse, suffering from high fever and periods of some delusion.
I feel incredibly selfish that while I am concerned greatly for my dear friend, my thoughts are with Jonathan and why I've not heard from him.
Quincey has become a close confident, and he is so very different than Jon, no doubt owing to his American West upbringing. He is truly a cowboy straight out of dime novels.
The air here is thick with moisture as if a storm is about to break, and everyone seems to be on the edge of a raw nerve, Mrs. Westenra seems frantic, and poor Arthur has to contend not only with the illness of his fiancée but his own father as well.
He recently got word that it is only a matter of time for him. I've learned he is a **British lord** and Arthur will assume the title when he passes.
Dr. Seward is doing his best, but nothing seems to work as Lucy's condition only grows more serious.
Perhaps all this frantic thought is causing my recent nightmares?

THIS IS MORE THAN JUST FEVER, MY LOVELY LUCY, THIS IS BEYOND ME.
ARTHUR...
I'VE TELEGRAMED MY OLD MENTOR AND HE AGREED TO RUSH HERE RIGHT AWAY. I WILL BE FOREVER GRATEFUL TO...
Professor Abraham VAN HELSING
CAN I HELP YOU SIR?
THIS IS THE WESTENRA ESTATE, NO? I AM HERE ON INVITE OF DOCTOR JACK SEWARD.
WHERE IS MY FRIEND JACK?

OH QUINCEY! QUINCEY! GREAT NEWS!
I'M SO SO HAPPY!
AFTERNOON, MISS MINA. MISS LUCY FEELING BETTER?
NO THE POOR THING IS STILL FEVERISH.
IVE HEARD FROM JON! WELL, FROM THE WOMAN CARING FOR HIM. HE'S BEEN QUITE ILL!
BUT HE'S OKAY!
OH?
THAT'S UM, GREAT, MINA.
WELL, WHOEVER THIS SISTER AGATHA IS SHE SEEMS TO HAVE THINGS WELL IN HAND, I'M SURE HE'LL BE BACK SOON.
I'M LEAVING RIGHT NOW TO GET HIM. I'M SO HAPPY!
"JON HAS BEEN SUCH A JOY TO HAVE HERE WITH US."
I'M CERTAIN HE'S WON THEIR HEARTS!
I MAY HAVE TROUBLE PULLING HIM AWAY FROM THEM!
YES...
...GO AND PULL HIM... AWAY...
...MINA.

I DON'T KNOW HOW MUCH MORE OF THIS I CAN TAKE, JACK.
MY FATHER ON HIS DEATHBED AND NOW THIS ILLNESS WITH LUCY.
I DON'T MEAN TO QUESTION YOUR JUDGMENT BUT SOME OF HIS METHODS...
HE'S BRILLIANT, ART.
YOU KNOW HOW I FEEL ABOUT LUCY.
DO YOU THINK I WOULD TURN TO ANYONE BUT THE VERY BEST?
IT'S JUST THAT...
PROFESSOR VAN HELSING! HOW IS LUCY?
FRIEND JACK, SHE IS VERY SICK.
BUT THE GARLIC AND FLOWERS YOU'VE FILLED LUCY'S ROOM WITH, ARE THEY REALLY NEEDED?
NEEDED?!
ACH!
NO, NO WAS NOT NEEDED, WAS VITAL.
MRS. WESTENRA REMOVED THEM DURING THE NIGHT, DESPITE MY ORDERS NOT TO.
SHE HAS ENDANGERED MISS LUCY'S LIFE.
NOW WE FACE THE DIRE RESULTS.

ARTHUR, TELL ME, AM I DYING?
I FEEL SO STRANGE.
OF COURSE NOT, LUCY!
DON'T BE RIDICULOUS!
WE'RE LOOKING AFTER YOU, LUCY.
SHE COULDN'T BREATHE LAST NIGHT.
THE SMELL OF FLOWERS WAS SO STRONG IN HERE I OPENED THE WINDOW.
I'M SURE THE FRESH AIR DID NO HARM.
IT DID NOT DO GOOD, MRS. WESTENRA, IN FACT IT CAUSED QUITE A BIT OF HARM.
DR. VAN HELSING PLEASE!
WE ARE FACED WITH GRAVE MATTERS BECAUSE MY ORDERS WERE NOT FOLLOWED!
WE MUST PERFORM TRANSFUSION.
A TRANSFUSION?!
I THINK THAT'S A BIT DRASTIC!
DRASTIC MEASURES ARE NOW NEEDED.
YOU WANT TO SAVE HER, YES?
OF COURSE.
THEN ROLL UP YOUR SLEEVE AND LIE DOWN.

YOU ARE A BRAVE GIRL MISS LUCY.
AM I DYING, PROFESSOR?
YOU MAY DIE, MISS.
BUT I PROMISE TO DO ALL I CAN.
THANK YOU.
YOU ARE A DEAR MAN.
JACK...
I TRUST HIM, ART.
JACK, PREPARE MR. HOLMWOOD, AND THEN SEND FOR MR. MORRIS.
WE MAY NEED HIS DONATION TOO.
WE MUST PURGE HER BLOOD.
I PRAY WE ARE IN TIME.
...MY LOVE...
...I'M HERE FOR YOU...

NEXT MORNING
ART, YOU'RE AWAKE!
I WAS JUST ABOUT TO TELL THE SERVANTS TO WAKE YOU.
WHAT TIME IS IT?
HOW'S LUCY?
QUINCEY, THANKS FOR HELPING US LAST NIGHT.
MY PLEASURE! NOW THAT LUCY HAS A PINT OF *TEXAS BLOOD* SHE'LL BE BACK ON HER FEET!
CLOISTERHAM PRESS
VAN HELSING IS WITH HER NOW.
ART...
...YOU SHOULD *BRACE* YOURSELF.
WHAT ARE YOU SAYING, JACK?
MISS LUCY IS DEAD.
YES, *DEAD.*
CLOISTERHAM PRESS
WOLF ESCAPES

MRS. WESTENRA HAS DIED AS WELL.
HER HEART WASN'T STRONG ENOUGH FOR SUCH TRAGEDY.
AT LEAST SHE IS AT PEACE.
NOT SO, ALAS! NOT SO.
AND THERE IS FURTHER BAD NEWS.
WHAT DO YOU MEAN?
DEAR GOD!
EASY ART, I'VE GOT YOU!
THIS IS MADNESS, PROFESSOR!
IMPOSSIBLE TO EVEN FATHOM.
BEFORE WE GIVE IN TO GRIEF WE MUST TAKE ACTION.
FRIEND JACK, I NEED A LARGE SURGICAL SAW.
WE MUST REMOVE BOTH HER HEAD AND HEART.
WE MUST ACT BEFORE...
PROFESSOR!
NO!
WE WILL NOT...MALIGN... LUCY ANY FURTHER!

My Dear Lucy;
I am so sorry for running off while you were ill. I hope this letter finds you feeling better. I am happy to say Jon was well cared for by the nuns and we are heading back to England.
Mr. Hawkins has graciously opened his home in Exeter to us, but we'll see you in Whitby soon enough.
In his letter he said he considers Jon and me his family, I was so touched.
Jon is well, but very tired and not much for chatting. I'm certain his spirits will return once we're back home. I will tell you of our trip when I see you.
Much Love,
Mina.
OH JON, WE'RE ALMOST THERE!
WHAT SHALL WE DO FIRST?
WE SHOULD TAKE MR. HAWKINS TO THE FINEST RESTAURANT IN TOWN!
DO YOU KNOW MUCH ABOUT EXETER? YOU'VE BEEN THERE, HAVEN'T YOU?
WELL, I'M SURE MR. HAWKINS WILL HAVE A FAVORITE INN.
I THINK YOU'LL LIKE WHITBY. LUCY'S FIANCÉ IS NEARLY A BRITISH LORD.
79

OH DEAR GOD!
THE HAWKINS HOME, EXETER.
TELEGRAM
TO; LUCY WESTENRA, WHITBY
FROM: MINA HARKER, EXETER
HORRIBLE TRAGEDY STOP WILL EXPLAIN STOP JON AND I OK STOP SEE YOU THREE DAYS STOP
MINA
CAN I HELP YOU FOLKS?
ARE YOU RELATIONS OF THE DECEASED?
MR. HAWKINS WAS MY HUSBAND'S EMPLOYER. WE WERE COMING TO STAY WITH HIM.
FIRE WAS IN SEVERAL PARTS OF THE HOUSE.
TERRIBLE THING, JUST TERRIBLE.
BETTER COVER YOUR GOOD LADY'S EARS, SIR.
'IS NECK WAS BROKE. TWISTED ALL ABOUT.
SOMETHIN' 'EAVY MUSTA FELL ON HIM.
JUST TERRIBLE.

THE ASYLUM
BUT IT'S NOT PERSONAL, DOCTOR SEWARD.
I'M JUST NOT INTERESTED IN CONTINUING OUR CONVERSATIONS.
THEY NO LONGER PROVE INSIGHTFUL OR INTERESTING I DARESAY.
WELL HELLO! I SEEM TO HAVE ANOTHER VISITOR!
LUCY WESTENRA DIED. HER FUNERAL WAS HELD TWO DAYS AGO.
I'M SORRY TO HEAR THAT DOCTOR.
SHE WAS SUCH A LOVELY GIRL.
LOVELY, LOVELY HAIR, LOVELY... SOUL.
I WARNED YOU.

WHITBY
MINA! DEAR GOD IT'S SO GOOD TO SEE YOU!
OH QUINCEY I AM SO SORRY I MISSED THE SERVICES.
IT'S JUST GOOD TO HAVE YOU BACK.
MY HEAVENS, QUINCEY, HOW IS THIS EVEN *POSSIBLE?* LUCY, HER MOTHER AND MR. HAWKINS ALL WITHIN A WEEK!
STRANGE, YES?
MINA, MAY I PRESENT PROFESSOR VAN HELSING.
HELLO MY DEAR.
THANK YOU FOR COMING. THE HOUSE IS BRIGHTER WITH YOUR PRESENCE.
THANK YOU. HOW IS *ARTHUR* HOLDING UP?
MINA! OH I'M SO HAPPY TO SEE YOU. IS YOUR FIANCÉ WITH YOU?
HE'S... RESTING.
SISTER AGATHA MARRIED US.
CONGRATULATIONS!
MARRIED? YOU'RE *MARRIED?*
YES, QUINCEY, I AM.
ACH!
PANELLING
HAMPSTEAD HORROR
MISSING CHILD FOUND! SPEAKS OF 'BOOFUL LADY' OTHERS STILL MISSING!

HAMPSTEAD HORRO
MISSING CHILD FOUN
SPEAKS OF 'BOOFUL LA
OTHERS STILL MISSIN
THIS IS IT! "MISSING CHILD SPEAKS OF BOOFUL LADY," OTHER CHILDREN STILL MISSING.
THIS IS WHAT I WAS *WAITING* FOR!
WHAT IS IT?
I DON'T UNDERSTAND PROFESSOR, HOW IS THIS RELATED TO LUCY?
MISSING CHILDREN?
WHAT IS THIS ABOUT PROFESSOR?
THESE CHILDREN HAVE BEEN PREY FOR THE *NEW VAMPIRE.*
MISS LUCY IS THIS *VAMPIRE.*
WE MUST *FIND HER* BEFORE SHE STRIKES AGAIN. BUT FIRST, WHAT HAVE WE FOR *DINNER?*

EXCUSE MY FRANKNESS.
YOU CAN'T ACTUALLY BELIEVE LUCY IS A VAMPIRE.
THIS IS PLUM LOCO.
I DON'T JUST BELIEVE IT.
A VAMPIRE HAS COME TO ENGLAND TO CREATE AN ARMY...
...AN ARMY OF THE UNDEAD.
MISS LUCY IS HIS FIRST SOLDIER.
BUT THIS IS THE 19TH CENTURY!
THE VAMPIRE LIVES MANY CENTURIES, LIVING ON THE BLOOD OF ITS VICTIMS,
AND SPREADING ITS CURSE LIKE A PLAGUE.
WESTENRA
BUT ARE YOU SAYING LUCY IS RESPONSIBLE FOR THESE POOR MISSING CHILDREN?
MISS LUCY HAS BEEN CURSED, AND NOW SHE MUST FEED.
YOU HAVE THE KEY, YES?
DEAR GOD!
IT'S TOO TERRIBLE DOCTOR! WHAT DO YOU EXPECT US TO DO?
FIRST WE MUST OPEN HER TOMB.

JACK, MR. MORRIS, HELP ME WITH THE LID!
OH JON, I DON'T KNOW IF I CAN BEAR TO SEE HER!
CREEAAAAAAAAKKK!
KA-DOOM!
AH HA! SEE? IT IS EMPTY!
MY GOD! SOMEONE'S STOLEN HER BODY!
NO SUCH THEFT HAS TAKEN PLACE. LUCY WALKS AS THE UNDEAD!
PROFESSOR, IF THIS IS SOME KIND OF TRICK TO PROVE YOUR POINT!

WE WAIT AND WE WATCH.
FOR WHAT?
THIS IS INSANE.
LOOK!
DEAR GOD.
LUCY?!
IT CAN'T BE--!
ARTHUR... MY LOVE...
HOLMWOOD!
LUCY...
ARTHUR MY DEAR BELOVED.
HOLMWOOD LISTEN TO ME!
MY GOD IT IS YOU!
LUCY!

ARTHUR... MY LOVE...
NO! DON'T TOUCH HER! DON'T EVEN LOOK AT HER!
THIS THING, THIS CREATURE IS NOT OUR LUCY!
WE MUST DRIVE IT BACK— WE MUST DESTROY IT!!

BACK! GET BACK! BACK TO YOUR TOMB YOU SAD CREATURE! OF HELL!
EASY ART.
LUCY! LUCY!!
CALM DOWN MAN!
MR. HARKER, GET YOUR WIFE TO SAFETY!
JACK GET THE HAMMER AND STAKE FROM MY BAG!
DRIVE IT INTO HER CHEST!
NOW!
JACK! WE MUST ACT NOW!
THEN WE MUST REMOVE HER HEAD AND FILL IT WITH GARLIC!
NO!
NO.
I'LL DO IT.

BACK AT THE WESTENRA ESTATE
THIS IS QUITE A KNIFE, MR. MORRIS.
YOU PERFORMED ADMIRABLY, MR. HOLMWOOD. LUCY IS NOW AT REST.
CHUNK!
WOULD YOU LIKE WHITE OR DARK?
MRS. HARKER? MR. HOLMWOOD? YOU SEEM LIKE A DARK MEAT MAN TO ME.
PROFESSOR, AFTER ALL WE'VE BEEN THROUGH TONIGHT, AFTER WHAT WE'VE SEEN...
HOW CAN YOU EVEN THINK OF FOOD?
MY GOD!
WHAT MANNER OF MONSTER ARE YOU?
MONSTER?
LUCY BECAME A MONSTER BECAUSE I WAS NOT ALLOWED TO REMOVE HER HEAD WHEN SHE DIED. WE SEE THE RESULT OF THAT INACTION.
WE WILL SEE MUCH WORSE IF WE FAIL TO ACT AGAIN.

TO BE FAIR, DOCTOR, HAD I KNOWN *WHY* YOU WANTED TO... HAD I *KNOWN* WHAT SHE WAS TO BECOME...
YOU WOULD HAVE THOUGHT ME *MAD.*
IF YOU'D ONLY *TOLD* ME...
...THAT SHE WOULD *COME BACK* AS...AS... *THAT.*
I WOULD BE *SITTING* IN JACK'S *ASYLUM.*
THE *VAMPIRE* IS ABLE TO SURVIVE CENTURIES BECAUSE SCIENCE CHOOSES *NOT* TO BELIEVE HE *EXISTS.*
AS FOR THESE THINGS *"WE'VE SEEN,"* WE'VE ALL SEEN *STRANGE* THINGS.
HOW ABOUT *YOU* MR. HARKER? DID YOU SEE ANYTHING *STRANGE* IN YOUR TRAVELS TO AND FROM *TRANSYLVANIA?*
I DID...TAKE SOME... *NOTES.*
YOU DIDN'T WANT ANYONE TO SEE YOUR JOURNAL.
My name is Jonathan Harker, and I am recording these notes in my journal as a record of event my meeting with my client, **Count Dracula** tra through strange lands where I am clear regarded as an **outsider**.
I THINK YOU MIGHT FIND *INTERESTING READING,* DR. VAN HELSING.
The train into Buda Pesth ran several minutes late, but I was fortunate that the carriage for Bistritz waited for me.

THE ASYLUM
MR. RENFIELD, THIS IS MY MENTOR DOCTOR VAN HELSING.
I THINK YOU KNOW MISTER HARKER?
HELLO RENFIELD, YOU LOOK WELL.
J-JON?
MR. HAWKINS IS DEAD, JON. TERRIBLE TRAGEDY, HE WAS SO FOND OF YOU.
YES, REGGIE, WE WERE FOND OF HIM TOO.
MR. RENFIELD I WANT TO TALK TO YOU ABOUT YOUR MASTER, COUNT DRACULA.
I DON'T KNOW HIM!
NOW MISTER RENFIELD, WE KNOW THAT'S NOT TRUE. MR. HARKER HERE COMPLETED YOUR BUSINESS WITH HIM.
BUT YOU STILL HEAR FROM HIM DON'T YOU?
NO!
YOU KNOW COUNT DRACULA IS A VAMPIRE, YES?
HE CAN'T HURT YOU HERE, MR. RENFIELD. YOU ARE SAFE.
AAAAAAIIIIIEEEEEE!!
NO!
I WON'T TELL THEM MASTER!
I WON'T!!

I'M NOT SURE RENFIELD WAS OF MUCH USE.
NOT TRUE, MR. HARKER. HIS MALADY CONFIRMS THE FANTASTICAL NATURE OF YOUR EXPERIENCE.
WHICH HAS PROVIDED US WITH A WEALTH OF INFORMATION. NOW WE KNOW THE VAMPIRE...
...MUST RETURN TO HIS COFFIN EACH MORNING AT DAWN.
WE NEED TO DESTROY EACH OF THESE BOXES.
GIVE HIM NO PLACE TO RETREAT.
YOU KNOW THE LOCATIONS OF THESE BOXES, MR. HARKER? YOUR FIRM ARRANGED THE DELIVERY.
I KNOW OF CARFAX NEXT DOOR.
MY EMPLOYER HAD RECORDS, BUT THEY WERE DESTROYED WITH HIS HOME.
I DON'T RECALL THE OTHERS.
I TOOK OVER THE ACCOUNT FROM RENFIELD.
WAIT!
MINA DIDN'T YOU READ THE FILES ON THE TRAIN?
NO I DIDN'T JON.
NO.
YOU SAID YOU DID.
I'M SICK OF ALL THIS TALK!
I HATE THIS PLACE!
LEAVE ME ALONE!
MINA! PLEASE YOU'RE OVER-REACTING!
SLAM!
WHAT DID I--?
I DON'T KNOW JACK SPIT ABOUT VAMPIRES, BUT I DO KNOW ABOUT WOMEN.
AND THAT IS ONE ANGRY TEXAN.

LATER...
DRACULA LIKELY KILLED P.J. HAWKINS AND BURNED DOWN HIS HOME TO DESTROY THOSE RECORDS OF PURCHASED LAND.
BUT WHY WOULD MINA LIE ABOUT SEEING THEM?
YOU ASK ME THINGS I CAN'T ANSWER, MR. HARKER.
SINCE WE APPROACH ONE OF THE PROPERTIES YOUR FIRM SOLD HIM...
...I SUSPECT WE'LL FIND ANSWERS SOON.
WHAT I'D LIKE TO KNOW IS WHY WE'RE NOT WAITING UNTIL MORNING TO GO AFTER THIS HOMBRE?
AREN'T VAMPIRES MORE POWERFUL AT NIGHT?
BECAUSE WE CANNOT WAIT, MR. MORRIS! NOW QUICKLY, GO AROUND TO THE BACK...
...WE WILL GIVE YOU A MOMENT AND THEN COME IN THROUGH THE FRONT DOOR.
WE BEGIN THE END OF DRACULA!
DEAR GOD, THIS PLACE IS MASSIVE!
93

IT'S DARK!
WHICH WAY DO WE GO?
WE FOLLOW THE SMELL OF *DEATH.*
AND WE SEE WHERE IT TAKES US...
IS THAT A *COFFIN* UP AHEAD?
YES.
QUICKLY!
PRY OFF THE LID, THEN SPRINKLE *THE HOLY WATER* AND LEAVE ONE OF THE SACRED *WAFERS.*
HARKER'S NOTES SAID THERE ARE *FIFTY* BOXES, WE MUST FIND ALL OF THEM.
LET'S DO THIS!
WAIT!
DO YOU *HEAR* THAT?
WHAT IS THAT?

RATS! HUNDREDS OF THEM!
BURN 'EM!
THESE ARE NO ORDINARY RATS!

THERE'S TOO MANY OF THEM!
I'M AFRAID WE'RE GONNA HAVE TO RETREAT!
BURN 'EM!
WHAT THE...?
ABITERE LARVA! ABITERE!!
THEY'RE GONE! WHATEVER YOU SAID— IT WORKED!
WHAT DO YOU SAY NOW, MR. HOLMWOOD? DO YOU STILL HAVE DOUBT?
THE VAMPIRE CAN CONTROL ALL CREATURES OF THE NIGHT!
WE DON'T HAVE MUCH TIME! WE WILL BE ATTACKED AGAIN!

WE MUST PURIFY THE DIRT IN HIS COFFINS WITH HOLY WATER.
MUCH AS I DO ENJOY A GOOD TUSSLE...
DOING THIS DURING THE DAY MIGHT'VE BEEN SMARTER.
EVERY MINUTE WE DELAY THE VAMPIRE SPREADS HIS DEADLY PLAGUE.
BY MORNING THEIR NUMBERS WILL BE BEYOND OUR MEANS.
UH, PROFESSOR...
WE'VE GOT COMPANY!
BACK, VILE HELL SPAWN!
GET BACK!
I SAW SIMILAR MONSTERS IN TRANSYLVANIA!
I DON'T THINK THEY'RE VAMPIRES!
THEY CAN BE STOPPED IF YOU HIT THEM IN THE HEAD!
MINDLESS GUARD DOGS NO DOUBT!

JACK YOU AND HARKER GET THE HOLY WATER!
PURGE DRACULA'S COFFINS!
WE'LL HOLD THEM OFF!
DON'T DELAY!
GET MOVING JACK! IT'S ALL UP TO YOU!
C'MON HARKER!
GRAB THE SATCHEL WITH THE WAFERS!
WE SHOULD STAY AND HELP THEM!
HARKER...
IF WE DON'T PURGE THEM...
...THERE'S NO HELP FOR ANYONE.

THAT'S A FANCY SWORD YOU GOT THERE DOC, AND YOU KNOW HOW TO USE IT!
A KATANA FROM THE ORIENT.
A GIFT FROM A STUDENT.
I THOUGHT IT MIGHT COME IN HANDY.
OH THANK HEAVENS YOU'RE BACK!
HOW DID IT GO?
HOW'S IT LOOK?
MINA!
I'M GLAD YOU'RE BETTER!
I'M FINE.
JON, ARE YOU OKAY?
LET'S LEAVE RIGHT AWAY.
GET AWAY FROM ALL THIS MADNESS!
THIS IS CRAZY.
OH, DR. SEWARD, ONE OF YOUR CLERKS BROUGHT A NOTE, THEY SAID IT WAS URGENT.
THANK YOU MRS. HARKER.
OH MY.
BAD NEWS, JACK?
RENFIELD HAS HAD A SERIOUS ACCIDENT.

THE ASYLUM
FORGIVE MY RUDENESS, I'M AFRAID I CAN'T GET UP.
PROFESSOR, MR. MORRIS, DR. SEWARD. HARKER, IS THAT YOU?
IS MRS. HARKER WITH YOU?
YOU MUST TELL US, MR. RENFIELD, ALL YOU KNOW OF YOUR DARK MASTER.
HE DID THIS TO YOU, YES?
NO.
I DID- KOFF!
NO ONE DID THIS, I SLIPPED.
WE THINK HIS BACK IS BROKEN, SIR.
EASY. SAVE YOUR STRENGTH.
THERE IS NO TIME TO LOSE. HIS WORDS MAY SAVE MANY LIVES.
POSSIBLY EVEN SOME SOULS.
THE POOR DEVIL!
DID DRACULA DO THIS TO YOU, RENFIELD?
TELL US, MR. RENFIELD.
YES.
HE PROMISED ME ETERNAL LIFE,
HIS HOMELAND IS A DRY DEAD WASTELAND. HE NEEDS THE LIFE BLOOD OF LONDON.
THE BLOOD IS THE LIFE. I DEVOURED THOSE POOR CREATURES TO GAIN THEIR VERY SOULS.
FLYS, SPIDERS, BIRDS AND RATS. THOUSANDS OF RATS! MILLIONS OF RATS!
KOFF! ALL THAT LIFE, ALL THOSE SOULS!

YOU CAN'T BEAT HIM, HE HAS LIVED FIVE LIFETIMES.
KOFF!
HE IS THE PERFECT WARRIOR.
KOFF! KOFF!
HE RAISED ARMIES TO DEFEAT THE HUN.
KOFF!
BUT TRANSYLVANIA HAS RUN DRY. HE MUST EXPAND.
HE PLANS TO BUILD ANOTHER
KOFF!
ARMY OF INVINCIBLE SOLDIERS.
KOFF!
HARKER...
...PROTECT...
...MINA...
AHK.

WHY WOULD DRACULA KILL HIS OWN SERVANT?
DESPERATION.
OUR ATTACK HAS UNNERVED HIM!
YOU THINK HE BLAMED RENFIELD?
GENTLEMAN,
I HAVE A PLAN.
WHAT IS IT, PROFESSOR?
WE HAVE THE ADVANTAGE FOR THE MOMENT.
BUT HE IS VERY RESOURCEFUL.
WE LOST MISS LUCY BECAUSE MY ORDERS WERE IGNORED.
WE WILL LOSE MRS. HARKER IF WE FAIL TO ACT.
WHAT ARE YOU TRYING TO SAY?
I MAKE NO PRETENSE OF DELICACY, SIR.
MRS. HARKER IS UNDER DRACULA'S CONTROL.
MINA?!
OF THIS I HAVE NO DOUBT.
SHE IS SUPPLYING HIM WITH INFORMATION.
MINA WOULD NEVER DO THAT!
THE VAMPIRE HAS THE POWER TO CONTROL OTHERS.
BUT WE CAN USE THIS TO OUR ADVANTAGE.
WE WILL HYPNOTIZE HER...
WE WILL MAKE HER BELIEVE WE KNOW THE WHEREABOUTS OF ALL OF THE REMAINING COFFINS.
DRACULA WILL READ HER THOUGHTS AND THINK WE ARE CORNERING HIM.
IT WILL FLUSH HIM OUT OF HIS HIDING SPOT.

WHAT IF SHE DOESN'T AGREE TO BE HYPNOTIZED?
WE'LL CROSS THAT WATER WHEN WE COME TO IT.
AAAAAIIIIIIIEEEEEEEE!!!!
DID YOU HEAR THAT?
THAT CAME FROM THE WESTENRA HOUSE!
HURRY!
MINA!
THAT'S ARTHUR SCREAMING!
AAAAAIIIIIIIEEEEEEEE!!!!
DEAR GOD, HOLMWOOD!
FORGET ME!!
CHECK IN ON MINA!
GET THIS THING OFF ME, QUINCEY!
MINA!!
WHAT THE HELL IS IT??!
MINA!!! MINA!!
WHY ISN'T SHE ANSWERING ME??!
DON'T PANIC!
MINA??!!

OH GOD...
MINA!!
GET YOUR FILTHY HANDS OFF HER!!
HHHIIISSSSSSSSSSSSS!!!!!

HARKER YOU FOOL!
THWAK!!
SHE BELONGS TO ME NOW.
NO!
BACK DEMON!
BACK CREATURE OF HELL!
VAN HELSING.
YOU ARE WISE, FOR ONE WHO HAS LIVED BUT ONE LIFE-TIME.

HOLD STILL ART!
GET THIS FACELESS THING OFF ME, QUINC!
SHOOT IT!!
DAMN IT QUINCEY, JUST SHOOT IT!
I'M AFRAID I'LL HIT YOU!
SHOOT IT OR SHOOT ME!
HOLY—
IT'S...
IT AIN'T FACELESS, ART!
SHNK!
IT'S HARKER'S BOSS, HAWKINS. HIS HEAD IS TURNED COMPLETELY AROUND!
A SOLDIER OF DRACULA'S ARMY NO DOUBT.
MY GOD! LOOK AT IT!

DRACULA WILL HAVE AN ARMY OF THESE MANGLED MEN ATTACKING LONDON IF WE DON'T STOP HIM.
BUT THESE CORPSES ARE LESS DANGEROUS THAN THE VAMPIRE HORDES HE WILL CREATE.
WE MUST ACT QUICKLY! MR. HARKER HAS ALREADY SUFFERED A SHOCK-- WE CAN'T LET HIM SEE HIS EMPLOYER THIS WAY.
THIS WILL BE TOO MUCH TO BEAR AFTER SEEING HIS WIFE IN DRACULA'S EMBRACE.
IS MINA OKAY?
SHE IS NOT. WE DROVE DRACULA OFF WITH THE HOLY CROSS.
NOW WE GET TO WORK. YOU DISPOSE OF HAWKINS' BODY.
I WILL PREPARE OUR DINNER...
I HOPE YOU LIKE...

—GOULASH! I'M AFRAID I CAN'T COOK LIKE ***MRS. WESTENRA***— BUT PLEASE, HELP YOURSELF!
WE MUST HAVE OUR ***FULL STRENGTH*** AND GOULASH GIVES THE STRENGTH OF TEN!
MADAM MINA! I'M SO GLAD YOU'RE ***FEELING BETTER*** AND DECIDED TO JOIN US!
THANK YOU PROFESSOR. I--
--I FEEL SO ASHAMED, SO UNCLEAN.
AM I TO BECOME ONE OF THOSE ***THINGS?***
LIKE ***POOR*** LUCY?
PROMISE YOU WILL ***DESTROY*** ME BEFORE THAT HAPPENS.
MINA!
NONSENSE! YOU ***AREN'T*** GOING TO—
YOU ARE IN ***GRAVE*** DANGER, MRS. HARKER.
BUT THERE IS SOMETHING WE CAN TRY.
WE ***MUST*** BE HONEST HERE.
YES PROFESSOR— ***ANYTHING!***
YOU ARE WITH US, MADAM MINA, AND WITH HIM.
YOU WILL REMEMBER NOTHING OF THIS EVENT.
HE CAN READ YOUR THOUGHTS, BUT NOT THESE.
YOU MUST WARN HIM, MINA; WE KNOW THE
LOCATION OF ALL OF HIS COFFINS.
WE HAVE A SMALL ARMY OF MEN TO AID US,
WE WILL DESTROY ALL OF THESE BOXES, WE
WILL PURGE HIS SANCTUARY. HE IS
NO LONGER SAFE IN ENGLAND.
HE MUST FLEE BEFORE WE
STRIKE. DO YOU
UNDERSTAND,
MINA?
YES PROFESSOR, I UNDERSTAND.

JON HARKER'S JOURNAL OCT 24, 1897
Once again I turn to this journal which helped me through the darkest days in Transylvania, and now the thought of losing Mina is wearing on me.
Van Helsing continued to work with her, using the hypnosis, while the rest of us hunted for The Count's remaining coffins.
We discovered some in Piccadilly and one in Liverpool, but there were still nearly a half dozen scattered all over England. I felt it was hopeless until we arrived at the Westenra Estate finding Van Helsing packing his bags.
OUR RUSE HAS WORKED!
WE HAVE CONVINCED DRACULA HE CANNOT SUCCEED, SO HE FLEES!
HE HAS TOLD MINA HE WILL RETURN TO TRANSYLVANIA AND WAIT FOR US TO DIE OFF.
YEARS ARE TO HIM AS MONTHS ARE TO US.
WE MUST STOP HIM BEFORE HE RETURNS TO HIS CASTLE! FRIEND JON, YOU ARE FAMILIAR WITH THE REGION, YOU WILL LEAD US THERE!
WE MUST LEAVE—
NOW!

We divide into three groups.
I THINK IT'S ABOUT TIME YOU CALLED ME QUINCEY.
YOU'LL BE FINE, JON.
I HOPE I'LL BE UP TO THIS MR. MORRIS.
I ADMIT TO BEING MORE THAN A BIT NERVOUS.
Mr Morris and I head off first on fast hourses.
Despite my inept riding skills, we will reach the Borgo Pass quickly via a direct route through rough terrain.
WE DO THIS TO SAVE MINA.
OKAY QUINCEY.
Mina with the Professor.
MADAM MINA, YOU WILL BE FAR MORE COMFORTABLE INSIDE THE CARRIAGE.
WE ARE IN FOR A LONG AND TRYING RIDE.
She's decidedly different since we found her with Dracula. It might be the effects of the hypnosis sessions. I fear she may suffer poor Lucy's fate.
NO PROFESSOR, YOU DEAR MAN, I WOULD RATHER RIDE UP HERE WITH YOU.
I FEEL MUCH SAFER BESIDE YOU.
If we fail, that fate awaits all of England.

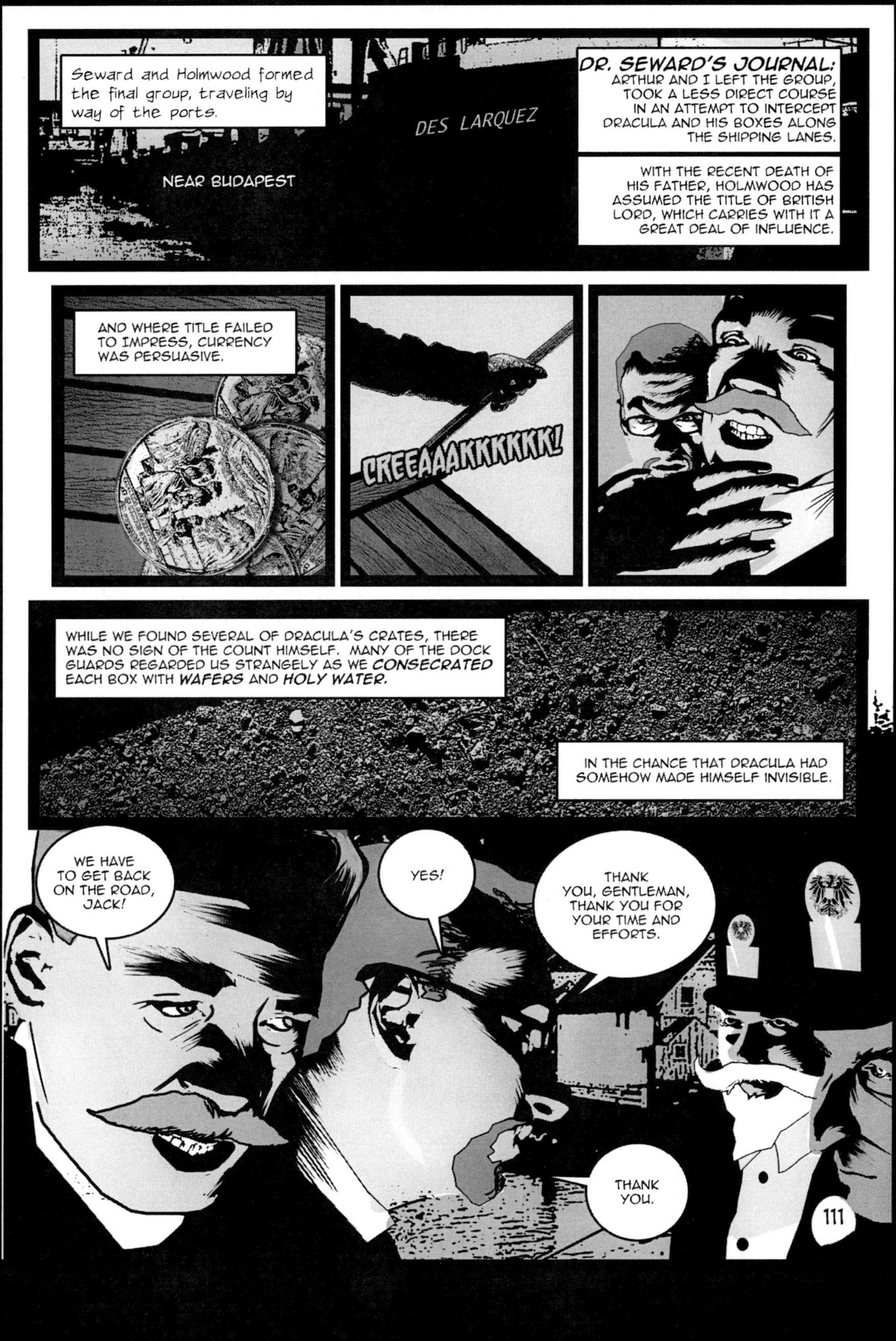
Seward and Holmwood formed the final group, traveling by way of the ports.
DES LARQUEZ
NEAR BUDAPEST
DR. SEWARD'S JOURNAL: ARTHUR AND I LEFT THE GROUP, TOOK A LESS DIRECT COURSE IN AN ATTEMPT TO INTERCEPT DRACULA AND HIS BOXES ALONG THE SHIPPING LANES.
WITH THE RECENT DEATH OF HIS FATHER, HOLMWOOD HAS ASSUMED THE TITLE OF BRITISH LORD, WHICH CARRIES WITH IT A GREAT DEAL OF INFLUENCE.
AND WHERE TITLE FAILED TO IMPRESS, CURRENCY WAS PERSUASIVE.
CREEAAAKKKKKK!
WHILE WE FOUND SEVERAL OF DRACULA'S CRATES, THERE WAS NO SIGN OF THE COUNT HIMSELF. MANY OF THE DOCK GUARDS REGARDED US STRANGELY AS WE CONSECRATED EACH BOX WITH WAFERS AND HOLY WATER.
IN THE CHANCE THAT DRACULA HAD SOMEHOW MADE HIMSELF INVISIBLE.
WE HAVE TO GET BACK ON THE ROAD, JACK!
YES!
THANK YOU, GENTLEMAN, THANK YOU FOR YOUR TIME AND EFFORTS.
THANK YOU.

HARKER'S JOURNAL OCTOBER 31, 1897
Three days of waiting here at the Borgo Pass were nearly unbearable. It was a relief when The Professor and Mina arrived today, oh how beautiful she looked! I think even Quincey was smitten!
Van Helsing instructed us to hold our positions and wait for Arthur and Jack, while he and Mina went on up to the Castle.
I CAN'T BELIEVE WE'RE HERE.
THIS IS WHERE JON WAS CAPTIVE?
IT'S SO...
...BEAUTIFUL.
CAREFUL, MADAME MINA, WE ARE IN THE LAND OF GHOSTS!
STAY BEHIND ME.
WE MAY ENCOUNTER STRANGE...
...FORMATIONS...
COME TO US...
COME TO US ABRAHAM!
GET BEHIND ME!
BACK CREATURES OF HELL!
BACK!

I SAID GET BACK!
YOU ARE OURS, ABRAHAM.
NO!
GET BACK!
GYAAHHH!!!

I DON'T THINK A COWBOY HAT WOULD SUIT ME.
I'M NOT MUCH OF A COWBOY.
LIKE HELL YOU'RE NOT! 'SIDES YOU NEED TO REPLACE THE HAT YOU LOST ON THE TRAIL.
WHY NOT A HAT WITH SOME CLASS?
I'LL SEND YOU A NICE ONE WHEN I'M BACK IN HOUSTON.
I DON'T THINK A REAL COWBOY SPENDS HIS TIME BEING FRIGHTENED.
WHAT ARE YOU TALKING ABOUT? VAN HELSING SHOWED ME YOUR JOURNAL...
...YOU SURVIVED OUT HERE ALL BY YOURSELF! YOU ESCAPED FROM DRACULA'S CASTLE.
BUT I'M WORRIED, QUINCEY.
I'M WORRIED ABOUT MINA.
CAN'T SAY I BLAME YA MUCH.
BUT I TELL YOU THIS, JON.
DRACULA IS NOT GONNA TAKE MINA LIKE HE DID LUCY.
I WISH I COULD BE SO CONFIDENT, QUINCEY.
I FEEL SO HELPLESS WAITING HERE. WE SHOULD HAVE HEARD FROM SOMEONE.
I'M WITH YOU THERE, JON.
LET'S EAT DINNER AND THEN HEAD UP THE ROAD TO FIND MINA AND THE DOC.

NOT FAR AWAY...
JACK, LOOK THERE!
DR. SEWARD'S JOURNAL: WE SAW THEM JUST AS WE WERE GETTING DISCOURAGED.
THEY'RE RUNNING AWAY!
STOP!!
BLAM!
BLAM!
ARTHUR TOOK THE LEAD AND RODE FULL ON INTO THE GYPSY GUNFIRE. HE WAS LIKE A MAN POSSESSED. WE HAD THEM ON THE RUN.

I KNOW VAN HELSING SAID WE WERE TO WAIT AT THE BORGO PASS.
I'M A BIG BELIEVER IN GOING WITH YOUR GUT, JON.
THERE'S THE CAMP!
BUT WHERE... IS...?
MY GOD...IS THAT...
...MINA?
WHERE IS VAN HELSING, MINA?!
GONE.
NEIN, MY TIMING SEEMS TO BE PERFECT!
DRACULA'S CASTLE HAS BEEN PURGED, I FOUND HIS CRYPT.
AND HIS VILE BRIDES!
NO SIGN OF ART AND JACK. WE THOUGHT IT BEST TO REGROUP, DOC.
MINA! WHAT'S WRONG WITH YOU?
JON...
MINA! SNAP OUT OF IT!
COME TO ME, JON.
BLAM! BLAM!
QUINCEY?
I HEARD IT, JON!
GUNSHOTS! THEY'RE COMING!
116

QUINCEY!
BLAM! BLAM!
GET READY.
YOU'LL BE FINE, JON.
DR. SEWARD'S JOURNAL:
SHOOTING A MOVING TARGET WHILE RIDING ON A CHARGING HORSE WAS MUCH HARDER THAN THE PENNY DREADFUL ADVENTURES WOULD HAVE YOU BELIEVE.
I FINALLY HIT ONE, ALTHOUGH ARTHUR WOULD LATER CLAIM IT WAS HIS BULLET THAT FOUND ITS MARK.
WE MAY HAVE WOUNDED THE DRIVER TOO, BECAUSE THE WAGON SOON LUNGED OUT OF CONTROL AS IT VEERED OFF THE TRAIL.
BLAM!
P-TCHOW!
P-TCHOW!
THE SUN IS ALMOST SET!
WATCH YOURSELF!
KRASH!
JUST TELL JACK TO HOLD HIS FIRE!
I DON'T MIND DYIN' BUT I'D HATE TO BE SHOT BY A FRIEND!
HE'S A SHOOT FIRST ASK LATER TYPE HOMBRE!

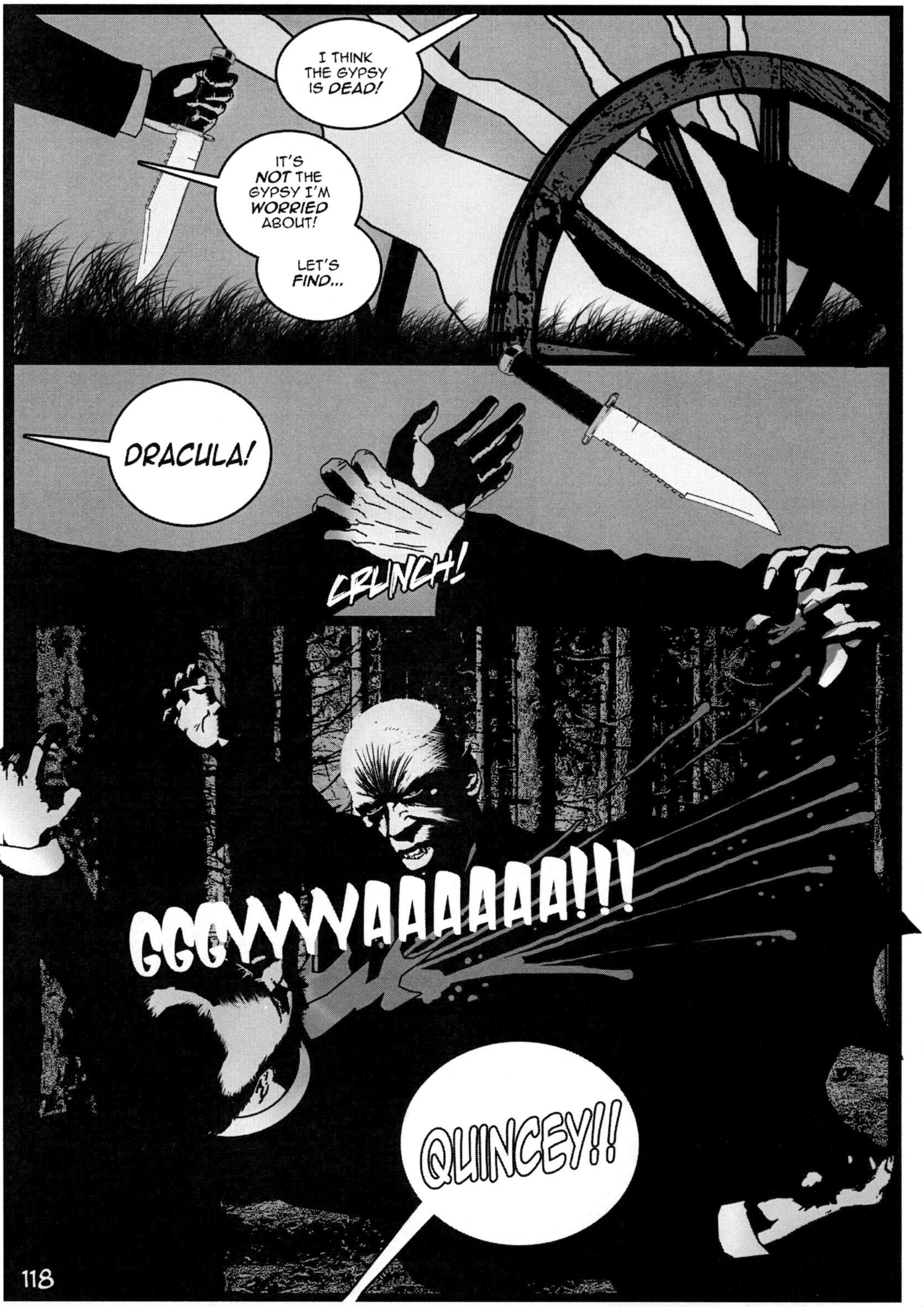
I THINK THE GYPSY IS DEAD!
IT'S NOT THE GYPSY I'M WORRIED ABOUT!
LET'S FIND...
DRACULA!
CRUNCH!
GGGYYYYAAAAAA!!!
QUINCEY!!

JACK! GET OVER HERE!
DEAR GOD!
HANG ON QUINCEY! WE'RE HERE.
HARKER IS THAT YOU?
I DID NOT THINK YOU WOULD COME BACK TO TRANSYLVANIA.
I'VE NOT SEEN YOU SINCE I *HAD* YOUR *WIFE.*

MORE OF THE UNDEAD!
PROFESSOR! WE HAVE SOME COMPANY!
YES.
DRACULA WOULD SUMMON HIS ZOMBIE HORDE!
YOU'LL HAVE TO HOLD THEM OFF MR. HOLMWOOD!
WITH WHAT? I'M OUT OF BULLETS!
TAKE MY KATANA! IT'S IMPERATIVE YOU HOLD THEM OFF!
I DON'T KNOW HOW TO USE IT!
WHAT IS TO "KNOW"? IT'S RAZOR SHARP.
JUST SWING IT AND DON'T CUT YOUR OWN ARM OFF!
ALL RIGHT PROFESSOR, I WON'T LET YOU DOWN!

IMPETUOUS BOY IN A MAN'S BODY.
WILL YOU CRY AGAIN HARKER, LIKE THE COWARD?
SEEMS TO ME YOU ARE THE COWARD, COUNT.
RUNNING BACK TO TRANSYLVANIA? AFRAID OF SOME ENGLANDERS?
DOG.
GAH!
THIS TIME...
...I'M NOT THE ONE RUNNING!
THE BOY...
...DIES A MAN.
CRITCH! CR-CRACK!

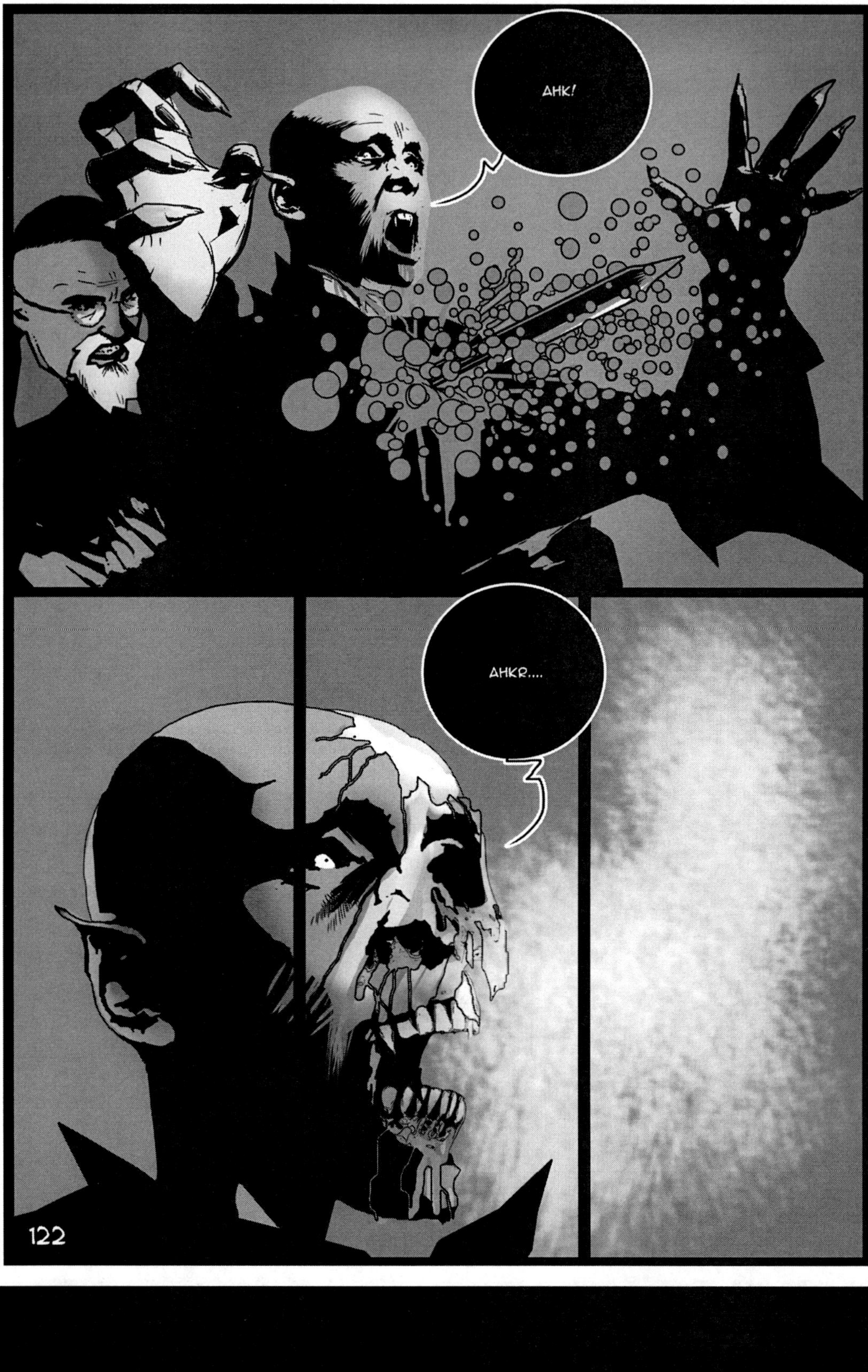
AHK!
AHKR....

JON HARKER'S JOURNAL Fully expecting a horrible death at the hand of The Count, I cannot express the joy I felt witnessing the professor's attack with his makeshift stake.
Van Helsing seemed transfixed as *Dracula's* impaled body shook violently, then turned to bone and promptly fell to pieces.
WHAT THE?
THUNK!
THUNK!
TINK!
His army of the dead followed suit.
WE DID IT! VAN HELSING, WE DID IT!
I DID ALL I COULD.
OH DAMN.
QUINCEY.
DAMN IT ALL TO HELL.
But we were not without casualties.

JON HARKER'S JOURNAL MAY 5, 1904 I've not written in this journal since we returned. Reading it now it seems like so much fiction.
QUINCEY!
DID YOU KILL UNCLE ABRAHAM AGAIN?
WHAT DID I TELL YOU ABOUT THAT?
C'MON MOM, HE'S AN INJUN AN' I'M A TEXAS MARSHALL. WHAT WAS I SUPPOSED TO DO?
'SIDES, HE TRIED TO SCALP ME!
YES! QUINCEY IS CORRECT! I TRIED TO SCALP HIM!
HE HAD NO OTHER CHOICE.
JON?
BE CAREFUL WITH THE PROFESSOR, QUINC!
Arthur moved to America, a British Lord living in Texas.
Jack has devoted his life to his asylum and his work, while Abraham has become like a second father to me, and a grandfather to Quincey Jr.
We lost good friends: Quincey, Lucy, P.J. Hawkins, Renfield, Mrs. Westenra, so many poor souls.
We survived but we'll never forget.

END THOUGHTS

DRACULA'S ARMY represents two years of work. My original concept was to produce a graphic novel of what I felt a more accurate version of Bram Stoker's original vampire classic should look like.

The hardest part of the process, for me anyway, is designing the look of the characters and finding the right style for the artwork.

My original take on DRACULA was much more cartoony.

Since I wanted it to be like a movie version I opted for a more realistic style instead of the cartoony one I originally planned out.

But I did know from the beginning that I wanted to base the look of Dracula on F.W. Murnau's 1922 film NOSFERATU THE VAMPIRE.

I recognize having DRACULA look rat-like with green skin makes him stand out, and maybe Harker doesn't notice, or is too polite to comment on his host's strange appearance.

Chalk it up to artistic license.

In Stoker's story, Dracula appears as an old man with a long white moustache who gradually gets younger as he dines on his victims. Visually an interesting concept, but I preferred the rat-like appearance of the vampire as he spreads his plague.

In some of the earlier drafts of the graphic novel I toyed with the idea of setting it in 1931 with Dracula helping the growing Nazi movement and setting the stage for World War II.

Germany enlists the aid of the grandson of Victor Frankenstein who has himself been working with his grandfather's creature.

There were a lot of great ideas in that draft but I let them go in favor of doing an adaptation closer to Stoker's original. I may revisit the ideas for a sequel but that will have to wait for other projects I'm working on first.

—thanks for stopping by! —Andy

McFarland Graphic Novels

Yellow Rose of Texas: The Myth of Emily Morgan.
Written by Douglas Brode; Illustrated by Joe Orsak. 2010

Horrors: Great Stories of Fear and Their Creators.
Written by Rocky Wood; Illustrated by Glenn Chadbourne. 2010

Hutch: Baseball's Fred Hutchinson and a Legacy of Courage.
Written by Mike Shannon; Illustrated by Scott Hannig. 2011

Hit by Pitch: Ray Chapman, Carl Mays and the Fatal Fastball. Molly Lawless. 2012

Werewolves of Wisconsin and Other American Myths, Monsters and Ghosts. Andy Fish. 2012

Witch Hunts: A Graphic History of the Burning Times.
Written by Rocky Wood and Lisa Morton;
Illustrated by Greg Chapman. 2012

Hardball Legends and Journeymen and Short-Timers: 333 Illustrated Baseball Biographies. Ronnie Joyner. 2012

The Accidental Candidate: The Rise and Fall of Alvin Greene.
Written by Corey Hutchins and David Axe; Art by Blue Delliquanti. 2012

Virgin Vampires: Or, Once Upon a Time in Transylvania.
Written by Douglas Brode; Illustrated by Joe Orsak. 2012

Great Zombies in History. Edited by Joe Sergi. 2013

Bushers: Ballplayers Drawn from Left Field.
Ed Attanasio and Eric Gouldsberry. 2013

Bonnie and Clyde—The Beginning. Gary Jeffrey. 2014

Dracula's Army: The Dead Travel Fast. Andy Fish. 2014